ENDORSEMEN

The person traveling two roads at once will get nowhere. The GOALS book shows you how to get exactly where you want to go, both at home and work.

—CK Wong, Google Program Manager

This book guides you through discovering what is truly important for your organization and provides a thorough methodology for setting and achieving meaningful goals to reach your vision. As a student and a facilitator of ***Business Goals****, I have seen the concepts successfully applied to organizations of all sizes, from sole proprietors to leaders of large organizations.*

—Jennifer B.

GOALS cuts through the shortsighted advice of hustle culture—work more, make more, never stop—pointing leaders towards the meaning and significance behind the grind. This book teaches lessons every company should ask, but few rarely dare to explore.

—Eric Zuidema, Chick-fil-A Operator

At the core of every sales training course I ever took or taught was the principle of "uncovering and meeting the needs" of the customer. The best sales professionals take that to a higher level, "find the pain and make it hurt." Jud's book provides solid tools to help leaders accomplish their goals, professionally and personally, by meeting the needs of the people in their lives. It is a solid read for young and established leaders looking for a tool to use every day for the rest of their lives.

—Don Horning, Managing Director, Worldwide Services, FedEx, Retired

ENDORSEMENTS

Business Goals *did more than help synthesize my faith and work-life; it helped build my faith by helping me realize that my work life is God's uniquely ordained mission field in my life.*

—Tony DeLoney, Senior Managing Director Investments, Marcus and Millichap

The business world is full of leadership books that take a single idea and draw it out into 300 pages of wordy repetition. This is not one of those books. GOALS is packed full of real-life application tools and points of action. It has become a go-to reference for learning to grow our teams and improve the lives and working environment of our people. You're gonna want to buy a spare to share.

—Jeremy Cappalo, Manager, Reliable Cadillac, GMC, Buick

I truly did not know how much I needed this book until I read it. My eyes were opened to realizing the importance of setting goals and sub-goals with my business team. We plan to utilize some of these strategies in our partner retreat to solidify goals and vision for the future of our firm.

—Kriss Mann, Partner, MUN CPAs

GOALS

Getting What You Want Most at Work and Home

Jud Boies

BUSINESS **GOALS** PUBLISHING

GOALS: Getting What You Want Most at Work and Home

Business Goals Publishing
P.O. Box 2661
Granite Bay, CA 95746
Businessgoals.org

Copyediting and production: Jennifer Edwards (jedwardsediting.net)
Book and cover design: Dave Eaton
Author photo: Bayside Church, Granite Bay, CA

ISBN 979-8-9860575-0-7 (PRINT)
ISBN 979-8-9860575-1-4 (EBOOK)
ISBN 979-8-9860575-2-1 (AUDIO)

Library of Congress Control Number: 2022906200
Printed in the United States of America

CONTENTS

FOREWORD

We all want success. It's a universal desire. The challenge is finding a way to achieve it. We've all been told that meeting goals is a path to that success. However, are the goals we are setting for ourselves ones that will satisfy our desire to live a fulfilled life?

Many of us may agree that relationships with those we care about are something that will last past any successes achieved in work or society. But, success in relationships is often as difficult to accomplish as success in business. We know where we want to be, but we don't have the right roadmap to reach our destination.

Jud Boies' GOALS is a roadmap that is easy to follow and makes intuitive sense. Cultivating successful relationships in business and at home will translate into better outcomes.

With years of experience in business, Jud understands people. He understands who we are and what motivates us. He developed this tool to help his teams become more successful and has now taught the program to hundreds of individuals and businesses around the world.

The tools shared by Jud are universal, regardless of one's business or career. As an elected official, I wasn't certain all of the concepts shared would apply to me. However, by using these tools, I have developed lifelong habits that will serve me now and into my future. I have changed how I approach life, spend my time each day, and interact with and lead my team. I am more purposeful about what I do and how I accomplish it. My life has more balance because building relationships helps me be more successful in reaching my goals.

Jud and the **Business Goals** program are helping me get what I've wanted most…at work and home. They have provided me with effective tools to help me get what I want, and I'm more fulfilled in the process. I encourage you to use this program to experience similar lifelong transformative results.

—Bonnie Gore, Placer County Supervisor, California

This book would not exist without the input and experiences of the people and companies who have deployed the ***Business Goals*** *program and the right side of the equation. It also would not exist without the contributions of Kurt Koch, Kevin Robertson, Alan Carlton, and Eric Bergen. Thank you to my wife, Mary, and my daughters, Paige and Kelly, and Caroline, for your patience, support, and for helping me live out the Goals program and the right side of the equation in my own life.*

1

RELATIONSHIPS ARE IMPORTANT

At some point in time, everyone becomes relationally unconscious, meaning we are absent in our relationships. Maybe not physically, but we become oblivious to the feelings and needs of other people. We don't do this maliciously; we just get distracted. Life gets busy, so we revert to task mode. Or sometimes, relationships get hard or stale. It seems easier to let it go, so we do. People are the driving forces of our lives, so being relationally unconscious is like falling asleep at the wheel.

Conversely, being relationally conscious is an awakening to the needs of others and responding to them. It is being learned in the art of relationship—not to manipulate but to genuinely care. Learning to be relationally conscious takes the blinders off so you can truly see the people you are working with or living with. When you do, you will begin to see big changes in your life, at work and home. The people in the workplace become more cooperative, your job becomes more enjoyable and purposeful, and your home life experiences harmony. You'll experience a change in your marriage to a new degree, and your children's attitudes will change for the better. Sound too good to be true? Become deliberately conscious of the relationships in your life, and you will see. New levels of success you never knew existed will be yours because it's not just you who will succeed.

The key to successful relationships is making sure we understand what the people around us need so we can meet our goals. If you seek to pursue, please, and meet the needs of the people around you, they will respond in a positive way. Then your personal and professional needs will be taken care of with a lot less hassle and demands.

There is an equation for understanding and accomplishing our needs, goals, and objectives. Half of the equation is determining what you want (goals)—this is the *left side of the equation.* The other half is determining what it will take from a people point of view to accomplish those goals and objectives (who)—*the right side of the equation.*

Left Side vs. Right Side of the Equation

On average, we spend more than 90% of our time and attention on the left side, so we become relationally unconscious because we only devote 10% or less to the right side of the equation. Then we wonder why we aren't successful at what we're trying to accomplish. We've invested time and energy executing the plan through tasks, but we haven't invested in the people who matter. Why is this?

I believe we don't know how because we became relationally stagnant. At our core, we are selfish. We're out of practice because the focus has been on self-reliance and accomplishment for so long, and we've forgotten how to pursue loved ones, genuinely please others, and therefore, have no idea how to tangibly meet their needs. Learning the right side of the equation takes away the guesswork. It will become easier to reach your goals when you can balance the left and the right sides, meaning we align what we want to accomplish with the people who can help us get there.

Because we are relational beings, we must focus on strengthening the right side of the equation. We need people around us to make our lives complete. Relationships are among the top two or three most important things in our lives. If you don't believe me, let me prove it to you. As a business consultant and someone who has taught about successful relationships at work and home for over twenty years, I've helped several thousand people come up with the most important things in their lives by running through three scenarios and asking a simple question:

1. You are on a deserted island.
2. You chose to go on a mission to another planet for several years.
3. You are the last living person on Earth.

In all three scenarios, assume that you have sufficient food, water, and shelter but could choose three additional things to have with you; what would you choose? What three things would you want to take with you that would be appropriate in all three situations?

If you'd like to take a crack at it, take a moment and write what you would take with you:

1. ______________________________
2. ______________________________
3. ______________________________

Every time I ask this question, I get the same three answers, but one of the top three answers is always people. (You'll read about the other two later on.) In every scenario, we want our loved ones with us. Why? Because we are relational—no man wants to be an island. From the moment we are born, we need people.

During the first sixteen to eighteen years of life, we experience a balance between relationships and accomplishing goals. We spend the first five years entirely with other people—parents, caregivers, and friends. Then in elementary school, we learn to balance schoolwork, chores, and spending time with our friends and family. But once we reach middle school, we begin to make decisions on our own, and soon acquisition and achievement become the focus. In other words, the left side of the equation starts to become more important than relationships and personal needs, which are the right side of the equation. Our quest for more becomes insatiable and takes hold at the expense of the right side. We become so interested in what we want to achieve that we neglect the people around us. This is what I mean by becoming relationally unconscious. We forget that we need people to accomplish anything, so we tackle things on our own. But try being married by yourself. Try being a parent when you're never home. Try selling a product without loyal customers. Try building a business without employees. It doesn't work.

This is not a touchy-feely book. The program explained is not a touchy-feely program. It's designed for anyone who has become relationally unconscious and would like to become relationally aware. It focuses on key factors that make relationships work, such as the character, competency, chemistry, capability, and contribution we all need to make things work. Focusing on relationships is a solution that works for home and at work. I believe you will enjoy applying the exercises and principles in this book because everything will begin to work more smoothly throughout your life. Your needs will be met because you help those around you meet their needs. ***It's the key to getting what you really want at work and home.***

In this book, you will learn how to identify and apply the right side of the equation through the story of Todd Hanson. He was somewhat successful but was tossed about by whatever life handed him. I wouldn't have described him as successful, really. He had no concept of how to have truly successful relationships, and things were beginning to go sideways at home. But his life shifted when he went to work for Blake Severson, a business owner who believed in the benefit of becoming relationally conscious because of what he learned through the **Business Goals** program. That's where he learned about the importance of the right side of the equation. Though Todd is a fictional character, every experience he has is real. I have witnessed the life of Todd Hanson through my friends, customers, business associates, and my own experiences.

The principles taught in this book come directly from the **Business Goals** program. It is a real program that has been introduced to thousands of employees and people over the past twenty years with remarkable success, and it's still being offered today. By implementing the ideas presented here, you can become relationally conscious and begin your path to true success.

I've set up each chapter with a chapter summary and some points to ponder. If you want to move through the book quickly, just read those sections at the end of each chapter. You'll get a pretty good idea of what the book is about. Have a question about one of the points in the chapter summary? Flip a few pages back and read the detail on that point in the chapter. I hope you will engage the material thoughtfully and come away with new ideas that can help you become a person who reaches their goals and dreams. For further instruction on how to deploy the concepts of this book, you can attend a **Business Goals** class or watch the video series. Either visit **businessgoals.org** or scan this QR code, and you're on your way.

Business Goals Class

CHAPTER SUMMARY

- At some point, everyone becomes relationally unconscious somewhere, at work or home.
- To become someone who is truly successful, you must learn to succeed in relationships.
- The key to successful relationships is focusing on the right side of the equation.
- The right side of the equation is about understanding how to pursue, please, and meet the needs of the people around you, so they will help you reach your goals.
- The left side of the equation consists of the goals for acquisition and achievement.
- This book provides a simple process for balancing the right side with the left.
- To better learn how to deploy the concepts of this book, attend a **Business Goals** class or watch the video series.

POINTS TO PONDER

- Are you more focused on the goals in your life than the people it will take to accomplish those goals?
- Have you been using people to accomplish those goals without regard to their needs, goals, and dreams?
- Is there an area of your life that is failing or weak?
  — Could this be due to a failed relationship in that area?
- Are you relationally unconscious? How would you know?
- What would it take to become relationally conscious?

2

GROWING UP IN AMERICA

"Your father left us."

Todd Hanson could think of nothing else. He had come home to his mom earlier, waiting on the couch, tissue in hand. She blurted it out as soon as he walked in the door. In an instant, his twelve-year-old life changed forever—he was stunned. On the outside, he stood motionless, but on the inside, he felt a blow to the gut. It was a blur from then on… another woman…an apartment on the other side of town…divorce papers signed. Shock numbed him, but then anger set in. He didn't understand how this could happen to a family like his.

The Hansons were known to be a great family. Mom, Dad, Todd, Mark, and the youngest, Penny, lived in the suburbs, the kind of neighborhood where the kids played in the yards while parents visited. Dad worked at a local tile plant as a shift supervisor, and Mom was a teacher. They made enough money to live comfortably, never experiencing real need. The kids got new clothes at the beginning of each school year and whatever they wanted for Christmas and birthdays. The Hanson's took a family vacation every summer and spent many nights laughing together around the dinner table.

Up until the divorce, life had been relatively simple for Todd. He'd known Grant, Cole, and Brian for as long as he could remember. Few memories didn't include at least one of them—catching frogs down at the river and taking swim lessons at the YMCA. Enduring Mrs. Parker's pop-math quizzes in fourth grade. Camping trips, barbecues, and raking leaves in the fall. They even had a secret handshake!

During those years, the boys would dream together, "What do we want to be when we grow up?" At one point, Cole decided he would become an astronaut. Brian thought he'd be a fireman. Todd wanted to be on television. Grant just wanted a Corvette. Even when life got complicated with parents or siblings, they were there for each other. There was nothing a close go-cart race or an afternoon fishing trip couldn't handle. Now, Todd yearned for the simplicity of those years before his family fell apart.

Divorce wasn't something new. Two of the three friends he had grown up with were in single-parent homes. His best friend, Grant, lived next door with his mom. His bedroom window was fifteen feet from Todd's, and the two often left their windows open in the summer, talking instead of sleeping. Grant's folks divorced when he was eight, and though Grant never knew it, Todd sometimes heard him crying for his dad in his sleep. Todd shuddered at the thought.

Now life was complicated. There were no more happy times around the dinner table. Family vacations disappeared. When he spent time with his dad, the girlfriend was there. To make things worse, Todd listened to his mom badmouth his dad night after night. Todd didn't disagree with her, but it was like picking the scab off a wound over and over. His grades dropped. He hated his parents. The fact that half the kids in his school had divorced parents didn't make him feel any better.

Think It Through

Was your childhood similar to Todd's? Did your parents talk to you about what was most important in life? How were your goals and dreams established? You may not have known there could be goals for your family, friends, school, etc. For example, your parents could have made goals, such as "We're going to work on our marriage this year, so we are both happy," a left side of the equation goal. But taking it one step further, this noteworthy goal could have been followed by a right side of the equation action describing what each spouse would have to do for the other to thrive in the marriage.

How do you think your childhood shaped who you are today? Are many of your beliefs, values, and current goals based on some of the earliest memories of your childhood? You once enjoyed spending a lot of time in relationships with your friends, classmates, and family. Has that changed?

If you are like most people, life has just passed by. You may have been taught what was right and wrong. Perhaps you were taught that it was okay to want things and that possessions bring happiness. But did the thought ever cross your mind about how people played into getting the things you wanted? It may have been a given that you didn't need to think about people because it was obvious.

How do you think the divorce between Todd's parents impacted the other areas of their life? No doubt it had an impact on their capability at work. They may have been competent to complete the goals of their jobs, but I suspect they were incapable of doing that job for many days or months while in the midst of the divorce. Studies show the average employee is 20%–40% less productive for the twelve months surrounding a divorce.[1] In other words, the crisis in Todd's life could've been avoided if his parents had focused on what was important.

MIDDLE SCHOOL AND HIGH SCHOOL—THE SHIFT BEGINS

In middle school, Todd began to notice a "status" and "pecking order" among the kids at school. It was the clothes you wore, whether you played sports, and who you hung out with that shaped your identity. His

---

[1] Rosemary Frank, "The Cost of Divorce to Employers," Nashville Business Journal, March 10, 2014, https://www.bizjournals.com/nashville/blog/2014/03/the-cost-of-divorce-to-employers.html.

awareness of the pecking order became subconsciously based on where people stood in relation to their acquisitions and achievements. The left side of the equation became the primary standard for measuring a person, not on who they were.

Todd muddled his way through middle school, coping with the pain and baggage of his parents' divorce. His freshman year in high school wasn't much better. His pain subsided gradually by focusing on other endeavors, such as football games, girls, and classes. He drifted through the year, rolling with the punches, looking forward to the next new thing. But in his sophomore year, Todd met someone who would have an impact on him. It was his auto shop teacher, Mr. Brooks, the first person Todd met who had some understanding of what it meant to be relationally conscious.

"Okay, men, break into groups of four and choose a leader. You have two minutes. Go!" yelled Mr. Brooks. The sound of shuffling chairs and chatter filled the room. Mr. Brooks pushed his glasses back, re-arranged some items on his makeshift desk, and glanced about the class. Todd moved closer to Grant, Brian, and Cole, and they agreed Todd would lead. The noise died down a bit, and Mr. Brooks resumed instruction.

"Auto shop is more than changing spark plugs," he began. "We will rebuild a car to compete against my other classes. These cars will be auctioned off at the end of the year, and we'll donate the money to programs that need it most. Your team of four will be assigned the part of the car you will work on. It will require planning, discipline, and teamwork. Your class could bring in the most money if you stick with it. It's a big deal to win this competition. There's one catch, though. You must have passing grades in your other courses to stay in my class. This is non-negotiable!"

Todd felt himself getting excited. He and his buddies were assigned the interior of the car. They didn't know a thing about upholstery, headliners, and gauges, but Mr. Brooks could teach them that. One thing Todd did know—his class was going to win this competition.

Mr. Brooks taught them more than rebuilding a car. He turned his lessons into a logical system for approaching any problem. His students saw the program, its goals, and the plan to carry it through. He broke the complex operation into segments and put a team in charge of each section. So that their work would integrate smoothly with that of the other teams, Mr. Brooks provided a formula for organizing their time and setting the goals needed to meet deadlines.

The sophomore year ended quite successfully for Todd and his friends. Their car interior took first place among all the auto shop classes, and their car brought in the most money. They had the prestige of winning the competition and received an award for their efforts.

In the meantime, Todd and his pals caught the car bug. Todd's mother and father bought him his first car, and he set about using what he had learned in auto shop to customize it, making it better and faster.

Mr. Brooks continued to be a major influence through high school. He made Todd and Brian his assistants, training them on the latest technology and providing access to the right tools. He then worked out employment for Todd at a local car dealership—his first job. Along with Todd's parents, he encouraged him to go to college. By graduation, Todd was accepted by a local college but decided on a school 150 miles away. Mr. Brooks felt it was the best school suited to Todd's interests.

Think It Through

Mr. Brooks understood what being relationally conscious meant. He spent an extraordinary amount of time with Todd on the right side of the equation. He talked to him about success in his life, man to man, even though he was in a position of authority as his teacher. He showed that he cared about Todd and positively impacted his life. He took the time to invest in Todd's life. He learned about Todd's interests, hobbies, successes, and struggles, and they spent a lot of time talking about each one.

Do you think this was rewarding to Mr. Brooks? Yes, and you will experience some of the same rewards when you deploy the right side of the equation in the lives of the people around you. But it needs to be deliberate. You must know you are working on the right side of the equation and not just let it happen. We are intentional about our left-side goals, but now it's time to be intentional about our right-side actions.

AN OPPOSING INFLUENCE SETS IN

Going with the flow of high school, Todd lived life day-to-day. His latest attention-grabber was an exciting new social scene. Todd's girlfriend was popular, so they were invited to weekend parties at the "in crowd" houses. Todd arranged for his three buddies to come along. Hanging out with people who had a completely different lifestyle than Todd boosted his ego. The biggest difference was the instant availability of drugs and alcohol. The parents of these young people, many divorced, had decided that all kids were sure to indulge, so they might as well do it at home. It would keep them off the streets, they reasoned. It didn't occur to them that everyone visiting the party had to drive there. These parties were huge and involved more than just beer. The kids gained favor by showing up with a bottle of vodka or the latest drug. As inhibitions faded, hormones surged. It wasn't really a party unless you'd had a few too many drinks and tried to go as far as possible with your girlfriend—or any available girl. Besides cars and their futures, Todd and his buddies now talked about how cool last weekend's party was, how plowed they were, and how far things got with their girlfriends.

Think It Through

Recognize the shift here? These parties were about what they could acquire in drugs and alcohol, who they were seen with (as a boost for the ego), and what they could accomplish in terms of alcohol consumption or with their girlfriends. It wasn't as much about relationships as it was about achieving. They were there for social reasons, so the right side of the equation existed, but it became overshadowed by the left.

As you will see, the left side alone is empty or, at best, far less fulfilling than the combination of both the left and the right sides.

THE FATEFUL NIGHT

Todd sat in the back seat of Grant's car, his thoughts racing.

It was a Friday night like many others. Someone's parents were away for the weekend, so that's where the party was held. They had a full bar and marijuana going, and then someone brought in cocaine. It was crazy—people were drinking, dancing, and the girls were especially affectionate. He was having a blast.

Cole had gone to the party alone and finally hooked up with Sherry, a girl he'd had his eyes on all year. They seemed to really hit it off and left together. That was the last Todd saw of Cole.

Rita, Cole's mother, called Todd about 3:30 in the morning. Cole had been hurt in a car accident. They suspected a drunk driver had crossed over into his lane. Todd called Brian and Grant, and the three went to the hospital.

At the hospital, Cole's mother met them in the waiting room. "Todd, where were you guys tonight?" she demanded.

"Uh, just a party at a friend's."

"Was Cole drinking?"

"I-I don't think so." He looked at his friends, unsure of what he should say. Grant and Brian just stood there.

A doctor, nurse, and chaplain from the hospital appeared. They led Rita to a chair and told her that Cole had died from massive internal bleeding. Sherry had been killed instantly. Though it was of little comfort, the doctor said Cole's blood-alcohol level was only .02. He probably had less than one 12-ounce beer.

How could this have happened? In the eerie, predawn light, they drove away from the hospital, numb with shock. Todd wanted to cry but held it in. He wanted to talk but didn't know what to say. He wanted answers but didn't know what questions to ask. He didn't want to go home. He didn't want to be alone, but he didn't want to be with Brian and Grant either. The only thing he was sure about was the pain.

In the end, they bought some donuts and went to the river—a place they would often go to hang out. How could Cole and Sherry be gone? This wasn't supposed to happen to teenagers. After four hours at the river, they headed home, realizing they would have to face their parents and the inevitable barrage of questions about the previous evening.

By the time he arrived home, Todd's mother had learned what had happened. A college student, drinking at a fraternity party, hit Cole's car. She was in pretty good condition with a broken arm and leg, plus some cuts and scrapes. But her life was about to change as she faced the consequences of killing two people.

Todd was surprised that neither his mother nor father asked the tough questions. Both were glad he was safe and figured it was someone else's fault. Todd and his friends had simply been enjoying an ordinary evening. To them, Cole and Sherry were victims of a tragic situation.

Todd knew differently, as did most of the people at the party. Any one of them could have caused the accident. Any one of them could've been sentenced to prison.

Eventually, Todd, Grant, and Brian returned to the parties. They had persuaded themselves that it had been a freak accident that had happened to someone else. It couldn't possibly happen to them.

There was a moment of silence for the two dead students at graduation. Todd wished Cole were there with him when he celebrated—at a party with drugs and alcohol.

Think It Through

This tragedy is not uncommon. Though this same event may not have taken place in your immediate family or with a co-worker, we will experience painful situations in our lives. How will you and the people around you respond? Todd, Grant, and Brian had each other to spend time with and work through the pain and misery that followed. In their case, it would be something they would never forget.

But how would the co-workers of Cole's parents respond to them? How would they help them through their pain, misery, and a certain drop in job performance? The changes may be so severe that they might lose their jobs. Wouldn't that just intensify the pain?

Todd was experiencing many realities of our society. He worked and made money. He thought he should acquire and achieve. He made decisions based on what he thought others expected of him. He had gone through a family divorce. And he experienced the pain of death.

With all those events, he still hadn't had any discussions about the most meaningful things in life. He still did not know how to live his life intentionally, focusing on meaningful priorities. He wasn't deliberate about much of anything. Life carried Todd forward.

Are your high school memories similar? Did your experiences help shape your character? The person Todd became was established between birth and the end of high school, yet it all happened by chance. Nobody told Todd he could shape his future and build lifelong goals while learning history and science. He didn't know there were important things in life that could bring fulfillment and happiness if he would build his life around them. He wasn't told there was a strategy to success. Most importantly, he had no concept about being intentional in relationships and the right side of the equation.

DO YOU HAVE A DELIBERATE PLAN FOR SUCCESS?

LIFE BEGINS AFTER HIGH SCHOOL

Todd allowed the summer after graduation to simply pass by. He partied most weekends and worked at the dealership during the week. He hung out with his girlfriend or the guys in the evenings. Life may have resembled some balance between the right and the left, but it was purely by accident. There was no plan, no objective, and no conscious awareness as to what he should be working on relating to the equation. He was in limbo between true relational unconsciousness and relational awareness.

At the end of summer, Todd broke up with his girlfriend, said goodbye to his buddies, and moved into the dorms at college. His first objective was to find a group of people he enjoyed being with. It was a right-side-of-the-equation need he had to fill. He found it in the fraternity system.

"Up and at it, Maggot! I need breakfast!"

Todd's body responded, but his mind took a few seconds to catch up. *Oh, yeah, rush week*, he thought. *I'm pledging for Sigma Alpha Sigma.*

It was an exhausting initiation process, but he did it. They accepted him, and it was worth it.

Todd liked fraternity life. It meant instant friends who closely resembled the group he was part of back in high school. It was a brotherhood (at least that's what they called it) that went beyond college. It met a deep need he had for relationships. Todd appreciated that Sigma Alpha Sigma valued academics, relationships with others, and high standards for how to behave like a man. These things were emphasized every day.

Though partying was hearty on weekends, everyone studied during the week. This was a first for Todd. He had never taken academics seriously in high school, but now it felt like the right thing to do.

By the end of his freshman year, Todd had a 3.12 grade point average. He had become active in the fraternity leadership and took the post of "Fraternity Philanthropy," the one responsible for leading community projects. And he had met a girl at one of the sorority/fraternity parties.

The following two years were a time of rapid maturing for Todd. He found a good balance between studying, partying on weekends with his fraternity brothers, and dating. He dated several girls and enjoyed the variety. He never experienced the same "puppy love" he'd had with his high school girlfriend. Even then, he had known she wouldn't be his life-long love. Hanging out with the guys was Todd's first choice. Dating was more of a necessity, allowing him to be with a girl from time to time.

However, the fraternity wasn't the best influence on how to treat women. When the guys got together, a group mentality took over. They focused more on conquests than the qualities of the girl. There was no such thing as a "relationship." It was more like "date them and rate them." For Todd, the fraternity came first. Hanging out with the guys was priority one. The talk was the same as in high school: the jobs they'd have, the places they'd live, the families they'd raise, and how they'd never make the same mistakes as their parents.

Back at home, Brian got married between their junior and senior years. Todd and Grant helped Brian find a place to live and plan the honeymoon. Brian had saved enough for a down payment on a small house with just enough left over for a week-long trip to Hawaii. During their time together, they spent a lot of time reminiscing about their childhoods. They remembered their conversations about what they would be when they grew up. They were growing up, and Brian was taking the first step into manhood. They also reflected on Cole and how he didn't get his future.

During his senior year, Todd realized he had accomplished a lot. He had completed three years of college, worked summers to earn money to help with his schooling, and became president of Sigma Alpha Sigma.

He had more than a hundred close friends he now considered brothers—well, fraternity brothers, which was as good as blood brothers in his mind.

As the year progressed, Todd interviewed with some of the many companies recruiting at his school. In previous years, he had seen many of his older fraternity brothers and friends go through this process and land great jobs, the first step to their job-home-family dreams.

Todd's senior year was a positive time in his life. As fraternity president, he had achieved real status. Many looked to him as a leader. He set the tone for the fraternity house and was well-counseled by the alumni who had been there before him. He built teams within the house to manage activities like cooking and cleaning. He organized a study committee that ensured everyone maintained their grades, a fundraising committee to oversee help for those in need, and a membership-building committee. In the past, individuals had handled these activities. Todd put at least two people in charge, with one spokesperson for each committee. Todd's practical ideas attracted a lot of attention from many alumni, young and old. He was experiencing a glimpse of success by implementing some of what Mr. Brooks had taught him, but it was being done at the subconscious level. It wasn't part of a deliberate plan. He had little knowledge about how to lead deliberately. But it was coming.

THE PERFECT LIFE IS JUST AROUND THE CORNER

Todd had a clear picture of finishing school, marrying a nice girl, taking a great job, buying a house, and raising a family. His adult life would be perfect, very different from the lives of his parents. As it turned out, he did meet someone during his senior year that he knew was perfect. Her name was Sarah, and she came from a very stable family. Her parents were still married and in love with each other. She had almost the same ideas about how and where she wanted to live and what was important in life. Todd found her very attractive. She was a senior too and graduated with Todd.

Todd debated between offers from the two companies he liked most. Both would allow him to be based in his hometown. Sarah was committed to Todd and didn't really care where he worked as long as he brought her with him. He accepted a job as a regional salesman for an automobile supply company called Regent Wholesale. He preferred this job because it related to his love for cars. Also, he worked with all the car dealerships in the area, including his previous employer, where Brian and Grant now worked. His job was to sell the consumable supplies used in the dealership's repair shops, such as batteries, light bulbs, and windshield wipers.

Regent Wholesale was quite large, with over 500 employees nationwide, and based in California. The job provided him with a brand new car every two years, an expense account for taking clients to lunch and sporting events, and a healthy income. It wasn't the six figures he had hoped for, but if he worked hard enough, there was a bonus plan that would allow him to make the amount he hoped for. He did his homework and knew that more than 60% of their regional salespeople made the bonus.

As a young adult, Todd continued to mature, but as in school, life just happened. He followed the path established by the school curriculum and then by his company. Before his graduation, his mother or father occasionally asked him what direction he wanted to take after college. This meant that Todd's life was guided by brief discussions with his folks as they tried to provide some guidance. These talks didn't discuss a plan based on values. Todd wasn't even aware that he should be thinking about such things.

Think It Through

Todd's sole influence was his environment—his friends, people at his college, the company he worked for, and the media who painted a stereotypical picture of possessions and achievements. Life was a constant comparison of what he had rated against what others had and what he wanted rated against what others wanted. Though it took many years, he eventually found that comparing acquisitions and accomplishments never leads to happiness or fulfillment.

Is this how your own life went? If you're still in the process, is this how your life is going? Take a look at how Todd spent the next twenty years. He was chasing the better house, better car, better vacation, acquisition of more toys, and other dreams, yet none of these things ever made a difference for long. They never provided the lasting fulfillment and happiness he was looking for.

WHAT ARE YOU PURSUING?

CHAPTER SUMMARY

- We start life experiencing the balance between the left and right sides of the equation—we spend a fair amount of time developing relationships with friends, and we spend a fair amount of time in school and doing chores.

- The shift in balance begins around middle school, when acquisition and achievement can influence friendships.

- Focusing on the right side of the equation should be deliberate in middle school or high school but seldom is.

- People don't know how to respond to tragedies—but they will through the right side of the equation.

- We tend to let life carry us along for the ride instead of being active participants as the driver of our goals and dreams Has this happened to you?

- We let society influence us more toward the left side of the equation to the point that it becomes the standard topic of conversation when meeting with our friends.

POINTS TO PONDER

- Did you spend a fair amount of time with friends and family until you were about eighteen years old?
- Did you notice a shift in acquisition and achievement sometime around middle school?
- Have you let life just carry you along?
- Do you have a plan in place that is deliberate about understanding the needs of the people around you?

3

TODD CHASES THE AMERICAN DREAM

With a great job in hand, Todd and Sarah moved back to his hometown. Using her Communications degree, Sarah worked in marketing at a local company. She was thrilled with her job, writing blogs and managing social media.

Todd and Sarah moved into an apartment together. They talked about marriage, but neither was ready for the actual ceremony. Maybe they would get married in a year or two. Each said they were committed to the other but wanted to settle into their jobs first.

Todd's parents were not supportive of him living with Sarah. At different times, both his mother and father had a conversation with him, encouraging him to make the commitment and get married. He didn't buy it. His dad had left his mom to move in with another woman, and his mom began dating shortly after that. What credibility did they have? Yet even though his parents were opposed to him living with Sarah, he knew somewhere deep inside that living together wasn't right.

Sarah's parents were equally disappointed. They had raised her in a home with strong moral values and had taken her to church every Sunday for as long as she could remember. They never said explicitly that she mustn't live with anyone before marriage. They simply assumed she understood this wasn't a good decision.

Todd's friends thought it was cool they were living together and told them so. This approval was an ego boost for both of them. Each had a great job, adequate income, and a live-in partner. Any initial doubt about living together was quickly overcome. Many people they knew were living together.

Todd and Sarah set up house in an apartment complex with several great amenities: a swimming pool, tennis courts, racquetball court, rec room, game room, workout room, a lounge with a fully attended bar, nightclub, and laundry facilities. It was the kind of place where many young professionals moved. It was almost too good to be true. Like college, the complex had a social calendar. Unlike college, they didn't have to study anymore.

They found that the class distinctions of middle school, high school, and college had moved up another notch. They remembered back in middle school when they had begun categorizing others by their friends, clothes, and activities. In high school, the pecking order had become stronger and more defined. In college, status hinged on where you came from or what fraternity or sorority you belonged to. Now, they had reached a new level. At every event, the topic of discussion was what job you held, what vacation you had taken, what brands you drank, and what toys you owned. Life was scored by acquisition and achievement.

They didn't realize that the left side of the equation makes no sense unless you have a right side to enjoy it with. Many of Todd and Sarah's new neighbors were single because they focused so intently on acquisition and achievement that their partnership or marriage fell apart. They became so out of balance that they lost their important relationships. They were beyond relational unconsciousness; they were in a relational coma, incapable of positive, conscious interaction with those around them. Now the best they could do was boast about their list of achievements and acquisitions in hopes that someone would be impressed and share in their success.

A SERPENT IN THE GARDEN

After six months in the complex, Todd noticed that several single guys seemed interested in Sarah. They'd try to monopolize the conversation with her or sit beside her when she was sunning herself at the pool. For the first time in Todd's life, he began to feel jealous. He was concerned whenever he had to be away for any period of time. When he asked her whether she noticed these guys were spending unusual amounts of time with her, she said she thought they were just nice guys who were lonely. His nagging concern continued.

Sarah finally learned that her "friends" were interested in more than friendship. The situation peaked when Todd was away on a business trip. One admirer ran into Sarah by the pool on a Saturday afternoon. During their conversation, she mentioned that Todd was away. After spending the afternoon talking, Sarah invited him to share some leftover spaghetti. After a few glasses of wine, he turned and kissed her. Not a thank-you kiss on the cheek, but a kiss on the lips with a much different message. Her admirer was starving to be in a relationship with someone and didn't care if it meant displacing Todd to get there.

Sarah didn't kiss him back, but she didn't exactly push him away. She was confused, so she thanked him and told him he should be going. After he left, Sarah sat on the couch and thought about what had happened. Deep down, she was a little excited. She was also a little scared. She tried to rationalize the situation. After all, she and Todd weren't married. She wondered if he might be interested in other girls when he was traveling.

Guilt set in the next morning. She had betrayed her commitment to Todd and let someone else think there might be a chance of more to come. She decided she had made a mistake. Her heart belonged to Todd. On the evening of his return, she told him they should start to think about getting married and moving out of the complex.

"What brought this on?" he asked.

"I've had some guys hitting on me lately. It's nothing, but I'm getting tired of it. It's not the best place for us anymore."

Todd doubted the reason but accepted her assurances. He knew if it weren't these guys, there would be others. He met with Grant and Brian and mentioned asking Sarah to marry him. He was looking for their approval. Did they like her? Did they think she was the right girl for him? Did they think marriage was good for him at this point?

The answer to all his questions was a resounding, "Yes!" They thought she was the most incredible woman Todd had ever dated. He would be crazy not to marry her before someone else stole her. Todd agreed, thinking of the guys in the complex.

ST. PATRICK DRIVES OUT THE SERPENTS

Two weeks later, on St. Patrick's Day, Todd popped the question. Sarah accepted. They set a date for their wedding—September 17. Naturally, their parents were thrilled.

The wedding was perfect. Almost 200 of their closest friends joined in the celebration. The honeymoon was near perfect, except the environment reminded them of the apartment complex. Cancun was a pick-up place for singles, a honeymoon spot for newlyweds. It was, in a sense, a relational hospital—quick medicine for what ails the soul. People went there to connect and work on the right side of the equation, but a week spent partying doesn't quite make it. Nevertheless, Todd and Sarah had a great time.

They returned to a home they had just purchased. It was in a nice subdivision in a decent part of town. Todd had done well in the first year of his new job and used his bonuses for the down payment. The yards were cared for by the homeowner's association, a plus for Todd and Sarah, who had full social calendars. They hired a cleaning service and told all their friends they had a cleaning person. What prestige! They had arrived!

THE RACE FOR ACQUISITION AND ACCOMPLISHMENT ACCELERATES

The first two years of marriage passed quickly. Todd and Sarah maintained a jam-packed social calendar, getting together with friends most weekends. Both were making great money and wanted everyone to know it. Todd had become the top salesman in his region. Sarah became the head of social media at the company she worked for and wrote her own blogs. When their combined incomes reached a respectable six figures a year, they moved to a larger house in an affluent suburb. They bought new cars. Todd struck a deal with one of his dealers to lease a brand-new BMW, and Sarah drove a convertible.

Todd and Sarah lived large and had the monthly bills to prove it. Their mortgage, car payments, credit cards, and living expenses absorbed every bit of income. But they were making ends meet and living a fast, full lifestyle.

By the sixth year of their marriage, Todd began to wonder what their next step would be. Some of their friends had started families, and that seemed interesting. They might have to cut down on their social calendars, or maybe not. Some of their friends had full-time childcare to maintain their work and social schedules.

Time passed quickly—the people they chose to associate with influenced their aspirations. Todd and Sarah had started their careers, acquired their first home, and made the money they had dreamed of as kids. They were playing the status and accomplishment game. Life couldn't be better.

Think It Through

Do you get caught up in what you can accomplish and acquire? Are your goals based on acquisitions and achievements? Regardless of how much money you make, do you still strive for acquisition and achievement based on what you can afford? What happened to the people in your life as you chased that goal? Were you making friends who were in the competitive mode of outdoing each other, or were they true friends, like Grant and Brian? Take a look at this next period of Todd and Sarah's life and see if you have ever experienced anything similar.

ANOTHER LIFE

"It's a girl!" the doctor exclaimed. Sarah cried out in elated exhaustion, relieved her labor was over.

Todd's heart leaped into his throat. Anne Christine Hanson, their first child, was born. She peered into their faces through wrinkled slits of blue and moved into their hearts to stay.

But Todd and Sarah were in for a surprise. Babies take work—*lots of it.*

They were accustomed to having their own timetables and assumed their baby would naturally work effortlessly into their schedules. They had not considered having to adapt to their child's needs. Diapers, feedings, and doctor appointments were suddenly taking priority.

Although they didn't get much sleep, the first few months were filled with joy. But Sarah missed her job, and both yearned to go away for weekends as they had so often before their daughter was born. They decided they needed to hire some help so they could get back to their old lives.

Through a friend, they heard of a service that brought young women from Indonesia to work as babysitters and housekeepers. After several weeks of paperwork and research, they greeted their new live-in help. The young woman's name was Rebekah, which they shortened to "Becky."

The couple took full advantage of having Becky on board and immediately began taking weekend trips. They arranged their schedules so that Becky did all of the hard stuff with Anne. The moment anything got messy, or Anne started to fuss, Becky would be summoned to whisk her away.

Life was so easy that Sarah and Todd decided to have another child for Anne to play with. Sixteen months after Anne was born, Sarah gave birth to Scott Cole Hanson. Sarah again headed back to the office as soon as she could, leaving Becky in charge of the kids and the house. In fact, she put Scott on formula as soon as he was born so that Becky could do the middle-of-the-night feedings. Sarah and Todd were getting a full night's sleep as if nothing had happened. They saw Scott and Anne in the mornings and evenings, although they left for work most mornings before the kids were awake. It was just the beginning of relational unconsciousness with their children.

CHAPTER SUMMARY

- Sometimes people focus so intently on acquisition and achievement that they lose sight of the important relationships in their lives and move into a relational coma.

- Sometimes people are so starved for the people-side of the equation in their lives that they pursue lousy behavior to get it. These behaviors may include extramarital affairs, unhealthy relationships at work, and lopsided friendships.

- We are all capable of striving for acquisition and achievement, regardless of the money we make.

- We become relationally unconscious when we neglect the responsibilities we have toward others.

- When we finally realize we've become relationally unconscious and reach the failure state (break-ups, divorces, separations), we tip the scale in the opposite direction and focus more time and attention on the relationships in our life. But often, it's too late.

POINTS TO PONDER

- What have you strived the hardest to acquire or achieve?
  — Did it come at the expense of someone else?

- Are you out of balance in any of the relationships in your life?

- Have you become relationally unconscious with anyone in your life?

4

A RACE THEY NEVER BARGAINED FOR

Todd and Sarah continued to increase their incomes, but there was always more to strive for, no matter how much they made. Their circle of friends was full of high achievers competing to outdo each other. There was always a better car, better jewelry, better clothes, and more extravagant vacations. They had to have something new or better than their friends or neighbors to feel good about themselves. Investing became a hot topic as well. The guys talked about what investments they had made recently and how they were doing. Even Brian and Grant had joined the race. Though not at the same income level as Todd and Sarah, they were still caught up in the excitement of who owned what—even if they couldn't afford it.

The three old friends and their wives still socialized, but Brian saw Todd the least. Brian and his wife often admitted that the Hanson lifestyle was far above theirs. Todd boasted so much that they were put off. Though Todd was his lifelong friend, he began to feel inferior. Despite his high income, he was just a mechanic. Todd was a "sales executive" and flaunted his title. Brian and his wife couldn't afford to give parties or eat in trendy restaurants on the scale that Sarah and Todd did. This division widened as the years passed.

Grant, on the other hand, had done almost as well. He and his wife both worked and had live-in help for their kids. And while Todd and Grant spent most of their free time together, their unspoken competition was friendly yet fierce. Whenever either one achieved or acquired something new, he quickly got on the phone to brag about it. Though they thought they were calling to chat as friends, deep down, each knew he was challenging the other.

Think It Through

Todd, Sarah, and their friends were running hard to compete, yet they never stopped to ask if this was a race they wanted to be in. Instead, Todd ran faster, unsure where the path would lead him. The left side of the equation is entirely about a race that can never be won. There is always something more to acquire and achieve.

Has this happened to you? Do you feel like you are in a race? Are you pleased with where you think it will take you? Do you even know where you want to end up? As you read more about Todd's life, compare it to yours.

ARE YOU CAUGHT UP IN THE LEFT-SIDE-OF-THE-EQUATION RACE?

A SEDUCTIVE MARATHON

Todd and Grant were competitive about their jobs, incomes, investments, houses and yards, clothing, what they drank, and where they ate. They were even competitive about their kids. Parents in their group insisted the children participate in sports from the time they could walk. This was another way to show off and spend more money. The kids had designer warm-up outfits, expensive shoes, and the best equipment. Some parents even hired trainers to help their kids get ahead.

When game day came, the parents were more excited than the kids. Each vied to out-yell the others. Some got so frustrated and competitive that they'd rage at their children for making a wrong move. The kids often left crying and mortified, convinced they were failures because they had disappointed their parents. Many kids really didn't want to play—if it could even be called "playing." Of course, the parents would never admit to being competitive; it was just how they expressed themselves.

WHAT ARE YOU "COMPETITIVE" ABOUT?

The junior sports scene kept Todd involved for several years, but he needed something new. Todd and Grant started going to the gym together and discovered that every good-looking single woman in town worked out there. All those well-toned bodies in skimpy exercise outfits. What an unbelievable spectacle! Both men were out of shape and self-conscious about how they looked but soon found their physical appearance didn't matter. As long as they had money and showed an interest in women, an abundance of beauties competed for their attention. Never before had so many women made such open advances.

It was the attention they were after. They had relational needs that weren't being met, and they longed for the right side of the equation. Somehow they had stopped pursuing, pleasing, and meeting the needs of the people already in their lives and vice versa. It caused them to think they could fill their need for the right side of the equation through other people. They were going from relationally unconscious to relationally stupid.

PASSIONATE PASSAGES

About half the women at the gym were divorced or separated and had become desperate to find another someone for companionship. The other half were unhappily married, eager to find a companion that found them desirable again. Then it happened.

Todd had a successful day. He'd landed a huge deal and was ready to celebrate. Several colleagues were having drinks in the lounge of the hotel. He joined them, ordering a gin and tonic. Several drinks and stories later, he found himself in bed with Terry, a woman he'd met at the gym who also worked at Regent. This was the start of an ongoing affair. Each felt safe in the relationship because neither wanted to leave their spouse, and they lived far enough apart that it made it a little difficult to see each other more often. Then one day, she announced that Todd was the guy for her. She would leave her husband, and Todd must leave his wife.

Todd was stunned. Though his marriage wasn't perfect, he was comfortable with Sarah. Besides, a divorce would cripple him: emotionally because he saw it as a failure and didn't want to be perceived by anyone as a failure, and financially because he wouldn't be able to afford his current lifestyle while supporting two families. His alarm turned to terror when Terry insisted they both leave their marriages to be together. He realized their relationship had to end and convinced her that their affair was over. Then he waited nervously for the vengeance of an angry woman, concerned she would go crazy and confront Sarah or blow up things in the office, which might cost them their jobs.

He was luckier than he knew he deserved. Terry decided to cut her losses and do nothing. Still, Todd confessed to Sarah. He wasn't prepared for her response, though. He learned she had been having an affair with one of his friends. Both agreed to try to salvage their marriage, yet both felt cheated and guilty at the same time. The following months were tough. Trust was gone. They realized they were searching for fulfillment but didn't know how to get it from each other.

PARTY HARDER

Todd and Sarah were soon to find themselves in worse shape. Todd dulled his emptiness with alcohol. He and Sarah had lived a party life for fifteen years, so it was easy to drink a little more. He'd often stop on the way home after work for a few drinks with his buddies. Once he got home, he would drink even more with dinner. He didn't know it yet, but he had failed to fulfill the right side of the equation, so he simply checked out.

They both tried to block out thoughts of the affairs and how messed up life had become. Their desire for fulfillment from other lovers competed with their outrage at being betrayed by someone they trusted. It was all too confusing. Instead, they tried to keep busy at work and with outside interests, hoping time would offer perspective.

They threw themselves into their jobs and activities at their new country club. However, the club brought a new set of problems and another level of competition. That was okay. Both were used to vying for position. The club's membership was a Who's Who for the area. Every prominent business person was a member. They all spent a lot of money on golf carts, lessons, and expensive clubs.

It was easy to get involved in something new and forget the pain of the past. Todd thought that happiness might be found in belonging to the club. Their intense schedule provided a positive, public facade, but inside they felt empty. They were together and doing the same things, but any semblance they had of a loving relationship was gone. They separated themselves from their kids. Anne and Scott were now in high school and wanted nothing to do with their parents like many teenagers. Todd and Sarah were so involved with their group of friends that they barely noticed.

Of course, Todd and Sarah thought they were ideal parents. They bought their kids whatever they needed and then some. They gave them lots of freedom. They didn't bother them when they wanted to go out or bring friends over, even when Todd and Sarah were out of town, which was quite often. Out-of-town nights turned into big party nights for Anne and Scott. They would tell the housekeeper to take the night off and have all their friends over for the drinking and drugs. Though Todd and Sarah set rules, Anne and Scott quickly learned to work the system. They had parents who hadn't a clue what they were doing.

STRIKE THREE—AND HE DIDN'T EVEN KNOW HE WAS OUT

Todd had tried it all. He had accomplished his career goals, acquired every possession he had dreamed of, and experimented with different relationships. Yet it still didn't dawn on him that he was going from one thing to another without any true fulfillment. He had no plan or purpose for the decisions he was making. He certainly wasn't following any rules. He had no idea there was an equation that could be followed to be successful in a truly fulfilling way. But that was about to change. Todd was about to meet someone who would change his life—someone who would enlighten him about the right side of the equation.

COULD YOU BE LOOKING FOR THE SAME THING? ARE YOU LOOKING FOR A CHANGE IN YOUR LIFE?

CHAPTER SUMMARY

- The quest for acquisition and achievement can divide family relationships and friendships.
- Society can cause us to think that buying more will make us happier.
- Acquisition and achievement can become your only link to relationships with other people when you call them to tell them what you've acquired or accomplished.
- The quest for more is insatiable. The more you get, the more you want.
- We all will crave the right side of the equation at some point.
- Sometimes we think the relationships we already have can be bettered, so we look elsewhere in an unhealthy way.
- When we can't fulfill the right side of the equation, we may turn to what we think we can control, such as acquisition and achievement, or just work more to acquire and achieve more.

- Sometimes we replace the right side of the equation with work, television, hobbies, and even drugs or alcohol.

POINTS TO PONDER

- Do you ever buy things you can't afford?

- If yes, why?
    — Is it to keep up with appearances?
    — Is it because acquiring things and achieving feels good?
    — Are acquisition and achievement ever truly fulfilling?

- Have you ever let financial ability come between you and someone else?

- When relationships in your life have not gone well, what have you replaced them with?

5

AN IRRESISTIBLE OFFER

Todd had been with the auto parts company for over nineteen years. He became a regional vice president in charge of fifteen regions. His area was continually the top producer in the country, and Todd was doing exceptionally well financially. He had his job so wired it was second nature. His life was on autopilot.

Then one day, Todd was invited to lunch with Severson Systems, one of the major manufacturers his company represented. He assumed this was one of the usual "you're doing a great job for us" lunches. Instead, it turned out to be a recruiting lunch. Besides President Blake Severson II, the marketing and operations vice presidents were also there. Todd learned they were considering him for Regional Sales Manager, a position similar to his current job and one he knew he could do well. Todd was offered other jobs in the past but turned them down. He was comfortable where he was. But what caught Todd's interest was an idea Mr. Severson explained that resonated within him.

"A job with us, Hanson," he boasted, "isn't about money or climbing ladders. It's about being *relationally conscious* and caring about others more than ourselves. We've found that everyone thrives when we strive to understand what all parties want and need and then seek to fulfill them. Our customers want something more than just our product. Our employees wish for something more than just collecting a paycheck. Our spouses want for something more than just a roommate. Our kids wish for something more than just a parental dictator. Everyone wants something more than what you think they are there for.

"We've learned that employees want to do well in their position while enjoying the people they work with. They want others to be what I call 'relationally conscious.' We've deployed a specific method to teach people how to do this through the **Business Goals** program, which incorporates something most people and companies are unaware of—the right side of the equation. The right side of the equation focuses on the number one thing people want in the workplace—*to enjoy the people they work with.* When people become relationally conscious, they become content in their work and personal lives."

Blake explained more about the program and why Severson Systems was flourishing. Todd was skeptical but intrigued. He thought it deserved further investigation and agreed to take a deeper look at the company. He thanked his hosts and scheduled a full-day appointment the following week at their factory.

Todd left the lunch contemplating this **Business Goals** program and this thing about being relationally conscious. He had focused on his achievements and positions all his life, socially and financially. The thought never crossed his mind that customers might want more than just buying his products. He was perplexed by the notion that his wife and kids might want something more. It made sense on one level because he felt he wanted something more from his family. But what exactly he wanted or could give was a mystery.

He wanted to talk about his lunch with someone, but whom? He decided to call Sarah at her office. She was surprised to get a call from him during the day and even more surprised to hear that he was interested in a new job. Things were stable and profitable for him at Regent Wholesale. Why change now?

Over dinner that night, Todd told Sarah how Blake Severson had caught his interest by the way he described his company's success. Todd knew that Severson Systems was extremely profitable. He knew all the people at his level made very handsome incomes.

In the past, Todd had won elaborate trips offered as sales promotion prizes by Severson Systems. Todd and Sarah met Mr. Severson and many of the company's regional managers on these excursions. They even speculated about what contributed to Severson System's success. Todd knew that the person he might be replacing made a respectable income, certainly more than Todd was currently earning for doing essentially the same job.

Sarah listened as Todd explained the concept of relational consciousness. "Blake explained that people want something more than just doing business. Employees want more than a paycheck, customers want more than products to purchase, etc. Then he talked about how we want more from the relationships in our personal lives. Severson said he had a specific plan in place to achieve this. I would have to learn and implement this plan if I went to work for him."

WHY ARE THEY SMILING?

The following week, Todd spent a day at Severson Systems headquarters. He was greeted with a sign that read, "Severson Systems Welcomes Todd Hanson"—a nice touch that immediately made him feel comfortable and significant.

"Mr. Severson will be right with you," the receptionist said. She offered him something to drink and a binder with his name printed on the front—*another nice touch,* he thought. Inside was literature about the company, an organizational chart, and a section with what appeared to be several company policies and memos to their employees. He learned quite a bit about Severson Systems in the next few minutes before Mr. Severson appeared.

"Hey, Todd, how ya doing? Great to have you here!" Shaking hands, he suggested Todd call him Blake and asked if he had looked over the day's agenda in his notebook. Todd hadn't seen that sheet and quickly pulled it out. The day began with an introduction to the administrative offices, then a plant tour, followed by lunch with Mr. Severson, and golf with key personnel.

Mr. Severson started by introducing the receptionist and went systematically through the twenty-five people in the administrative offices. Todd thought this seemed like a small staff for a company that grossed several hundred million in revenue annually. He noticed the atmosphere was relaxed, cordial. No one seemed to be working too hard or was too stressed.

The employees called Mr. Severson "Blake," and he introduced people by saying something about their personal lives, along with a compliment for what they'd done for the company. Todd was a bit skeptical about the overt friendliness. Was Severson putting on a front to impress him? Did he really believe every person was doing that great a job? Was he sincerely interested in their personal lives? If it was genuine, it was pretty cool. But still, he was somewhat skeptical. He needed to learn more before believing that Blake Severson actually had that kind of relationship with his employees.

Next, they toured the factory across the street from the administrative offices. Blake introduced Todd to the employees at each workstation and the people they passed. Again, he mentioned something about the employee's family or personal interests and commented about a recent work achievement for nearly everyone they encountered.

Todd marveled at how well-kept the factory looked when Blake commented that everyone took great pride in running a clean operation. The factory supervisor was meticulous about having systems in place that required everything to be in exact order.

They visited the shipping area, where Todd noticed something else unusual. It appeared the entire administrative staff had crossed the street to pack boxes! Blake explained that a customer had an emergency and needed a large order shipped within the next few hours. Almost every administrator and supervisor Todd met were now putting boxes into cases and cases onto pallets. What's more, they looked like they were having a good time! Blake explained how when anything extraordinary came up, everyone pitched in to get it done. He rarely had to ask for help—his people naturally sensed the need and acted upon it.

THE BUSINESS GOALS PROGRAM AND THE RIGHT SIDE OF THE EQUATION

They returned to Blake's office, where lunch had been set up at a small corner table. The room was large and friendly, with many photos of Blake's family and company employees. While they ate, Blake asked Todd a series of deliberate questions to assess his abilities and attitude. He further asked if he had a set of written goals for work and home, to which Todd indicated he only had written goals at Regent. Blake asked how he ran his sales division at Regent, how many employees reported to him, and his management style to see if Todd had the competency to take the job. Blake then described the program he had implemented at Severson Systems, the **Business Goals** program, and the right side of the equation. He was mainly looking to see if Todd was teachable. Was he open to the **Business Goals** program, and could he implement it?

"The program we've deployed has many attributes of a game," Blake explained. "It is responsible for the success we've experienced at Severson Systems and for the happiness and accomplishment of every employee here, including me. I tell people the program has many of the same attributes as a game because most understand the concept. Games typically include a purpose and method for playing, rules, and players. The **Business Goals** program is no different. It has a purpose, rules, players, and a defined method to how we enact the program similar to the play of the game. The object is to be successful at the job we do and enjoy the process, meaning we want to create a great experience for everyone associated with our company. This includes our customers, vendors, employees, and even our families. If you choose to join Severson Systems," Blake added, "you will have to learn how to deploy the **Business Goals** program in your department, and I'd encourage you to deploy it in every part of your life."

"Ok," Todd said. "How will I learn this program?"

"The best way I know of is to attend the six-week class. That's what I did, and it helped me tremendously. If you choose to come work here, that's something you'll do within the first six weeks after joining the company," said Blake. "At the same time, you and I will meet over the next few months so I can help to solidify the content and show you how to deploy it into your life." He added that the concepts in the program could become some of the most essential concepts Todd would ever learn.

"Todd, the **Business Goals** program and the right side of the equation takes the game of life and kicks it up several notches. It adds purpose for playing and a specific plan to achieve the homerun that comes from true fulfillment. The key component is pursuing, pleasing, and meeting the needs of everyone around you. That can only happen when you have a process to understand and align the needs and expectations of all parties. This is being relationally conscious. First, you must understand what those needs are. Most companies are focused solely on their financial goals and fail to remember that they need people to succeed. At some point, almost everyone becomes relationally unconscious. We lose a sense of the people around us and their needs. We at Severson Systems care for our employees and strive to meet their professional needs, so they are capable of helping the company succeed."

As Todd pondered what he was hearing, Blake explained further. "The great thing about this program is that I can always tell whether our employees are 'in the game' or not. If they are in, their lives continually improve, and they are being fulfilled. I know when people aren't following the program because they don't perform as well and are usually unhappy or depressed, definitely not living fulfilled lives."

Blake pointed at Todd's chair and said, "Most people who've sat where you're sitting now don't know what to think. It's okay if you don't fully grasp it, but I can tell you it works. We are succeeding because our employees truly love working here. I'd say that perhaps all of them are satisfied employees. They can reach some of their lifelong goals and at the same time become more productive and profitable. This is a combination I think every person and every company is looking for."

IMPRESSING THE BOSS

Blake switched gears. Now he wanted to learn more about Todd, especially about his family. What were his interests? Todd started with a brief overview of his career—how in his first year as a regional salesman, he became the top producer for his area. He described the dollar volumes he had reached over the years and his responsibilities as he moved up the ladder to regional sales manager.

"What about your family?" asked Blake. Todd mentioned he had been married to Sarah for eighteen years and briefly described her career and the advancements she had made in social media. Blake recognized her name, which made Todd proud. Then Todd described his two children as "typical high schoolers, mostly doing their own thing these days with their friends."

Todd was eager to return to what he thought would impress Severson. He described all the things that wowed his buddies—his housekeeper, memberships at the local gym, and a prestigious country club. He described his elite biker club and some road trips they took each year. Finally, Todd told him about his stock portfolio so Blake would know how well he had done.

"How would you describe your typical week?" Blake asked. *Great! Another chance to impress,* Todd thought. He stressed the long hours he worked to show what a devoted employee he was. But life wasn't all work. He spent weekends at the club playing golf, followed by dinner there. He did his thing, Sarah had her interests, and the kids did what they wanted. Each of them typically went separate ways.

"And what do you do on Sundays?"

"Sundays," Todd explained, "are typically for my Harley motorcycle group. We visit other clubs or take rides around the area. Sometimes we bring our wives, but mostly it's an opportunity for me and the guys to get away from it all." At the end of his impressive discourse on his achievements, Todd was satisfied that he had done a splendid job impressing his potential boss.

But Blake was unimpressed, although the answers had been more or less what he expected. It appeared that Todd was, indeed, relationally unconscious. Blake knew Severson Systems could bring tremendous value to this man's life and his family. The real question in Blake's mind was whether Todd could bring value to Severson Systems.

"Why would you consider a position at Severson?" Blake inquired. This put Todd in a competitive mode. As Todd calculated his response, Blake suggested he answer from his heart, not what he thought Blake wanted to hear. *What did that mean?* Todd thought. Taking Blake's advice, Todd decided to be as honest as possible.

"Blake," he confessed, "there's something interesting going on here. I'm not exactly sure what it is, but it's different from most companies. My wife and I noticed it before on one of your sales promotion trips. This company intrigues and attracts me. I'm very comfortable where I am and never thought I would ever consider leaving, but I just get the sense that something's out there that I'm missing. I don't know how to explain it."

Blake smiled. A homerun answer. He told Todd he completely understood the feelings he was having. Severson Systems was more than building products and making profits. Their unique methods brought both employees and customers to the company and are certainly what kept them there. Blake checked his watch and realized almost two hours had elapsed. They had a tee time at the golf course and should go. In the lobby, four men and two women were waiting for them.

Surprisingly, the golf course was public, though it was considered one of the best in the area. Todd had assumed Blake belonged to a private one. Then he noticed Blake's golf clubs. Not bad, but not one of the expensive sets he had expected.

They split into two foursomes, agreeing to switch around after the ninth hole so Todd could meet all six people. The three people Todd started with included the company's accounting and production managers and the operations vice president he had met at the recruiting lunch.

None of the people in Todd's party played exceptionally well. In fact, they were pretty bad, though they seemed to be enjoying themselves. They told Todd that they only played once in a while with customers and other employees. It gave them a chance to get to know people outside the office setting.

The production manager chatted with Todd about various things, none directly related to production. He talked about the team he worked with and how gifted they were. He mentioned stuff they did together outside of work, like fishing and hunting trips, birthday parties, and NASCAR races.

They all asked Todd a variety of questions unrelated to work. He tried to impress them as he did his regular group of friends. Obviously, he was a better golfer, so he let each of them know how they could improve their game.

At the end of nine holes, the groups switched. Besides Blake, Todd was now playing with the national sales manager, the man who would be Todd's boss if he was offered the job. The fourth person was an assembly line worker. Todd thought it strange that this man had come along. What could he have in common with everyone else? But as they worked their way around the course, Todd observed that no one seemed to mind.

The two new members of the second foursome asked about Todd's family and interests, not what he thought he could bring to their company.

And, as with the first nine holes, Todd outplayed them all. Nevertheless, all seemed to enjoy themselves and made sure Todd did as well.

They finished up around 5:30. Todd was surprised they were anxious to get home instead of going to the bar or back to the office. Blake saw Todd to his car, promising to touch base in the next few days. He asked Todd to look over the material in the binder, especially something called Value Discussions. "The Value Discussions are the basis for discussions we have regularly centered around the rules we have in place here at Severson. They are important to us," Blake told him.

Todd stopped at his country club for a few drinks with his buddies on the way home. Grant was there, and Todd shared briefly about the day's events. He didn't describe Blake's questions or the right side of the equation. Todd still hadn't fully grasped what Blake was talking about. Grant encouraged Todd to take the job if offered, based on the good things he had heard about Severson Systems.

When Todd returned home, he tried explaining the right side of the equation to Sarah. After dinner, he opened the binder and read through some materials, including the Value Discussions.

BLAKE'S REPORT CARD

The next day, Blake met with the same six co-workers who played golf with Todd. He asked each to make a list of Todd's strengths and weaknesses, putting them in a weighted and priority order. Each list rated the positives as important, while the weaknesses seemed repairable with time and training. On the positive side, they agreed that Todd was probably an honest person who wanted to do the right thing. He had been devoted and loyal to the company he worked for and married for eighteen years. Their lists of his weaknesses were almost identical. All felt he was eager to impress. They could see he had lived a life based on acquisition and achievement and hadn't been exposed to the **Business Goals** program and the right side of the equation. Based on their conversations on the golf course, they suspected he didn't have great relationships with his wife or kids. He might even have stayed married for appearances since his wife was fairly well known or to avoid the financial disruption of a divorce.

Blake agreed with most of these observations. No surprises. Then he asked if they thought Todd would make it as part of the Severson team. The position was open, and Todd had the *competency* they were looking for. He was well established in the community and would likely stay with the company for another fifteen to twenty years. It appeared to the team that Todd had *character.* Despite some of his faults, he was a likable guy. There was good *chemistry* between them, and they enjoyed their time with him. Based on Todd's track record, they knew he could make a *contribution.* It didn't appear anything was standing in the way of his *capability* to perform in the job. He encompassed the "5Cs" and would be a good choice. (The 5Cs are something everyone learns about in the **Business Goals** program. See chapter 10.)

The employees had seen many lives changed as they learned to apply the **Business Goals** program and the right side of the equation. They decided to give Blake the "thumbs up" for Todd to come on board—provided Todd was willing to go through the normal Severson training process and attend the **Business Goals** classes. Blake concurred.

A FATEFUL DECISION

Blake met with Todd the next day and told him the group felt he had promise. If he agreed to go through the **Business Goals** program and learn how to apply the program in his life, the job was his. Severson Systems had a probationary period that gauged each new employee's ability to follow the company's systems and the program. Todd's new financial package was similar to his old one, with every sales position's normal incentives.

Todd decided to take the job. Employees seemed to love working there. The company had an aura of success and a level of satisfaction he hadn't seen anywhere else. Todd casually talked with a few customers, and they agreed Severson Systems had the relational component that had earned them an excellent reputation. For many customers, Severson Systems was their favorite company to work with. One company stated it was the first time they had ever worked with another company that focused so much on the relationship side of things. Todd was excited about what the future would hold for him.

WHAT DOES BECOMING RELATIONALLY CONSCIOUS MEAN TO YOU?

When Todd got home, he was almost embarrassed to tell Sarah he had accepted the job. He wouldn't do any better financially unless he performed at an extraordinary level. He couldn't explain why he left one company after nineteen years to take a job that felt better. He told his wife, kids, and friends that it was an advancement of sorts. He was now a regional sales manager with a manufacturer instead of a supplier. It sounded like another achievement that could boost his ego.

He gave notice at Regent, explaining he was taking a position with one of the companies they represented. He agreed to make himself fully available after he left and could stay a few weeks to train someone if necessary. It was important for Todd to leave Regent on good terms because he would continue to have almost daily involvement with them. They were an integral part of his region and could provide a big part of his future income. Naturally, they were surprised and disappointed after so many years, though it wasn't unusual for people to leave.

CHAPTER SUMMARY

- Many people live life trying to earn more money and climb corporate ladders. They try to impress people and measure their success based on how much they've acquired, the cars they drive, the clothes they wear, their home, and their position.

- Most people live in the "default mode." They just let life happen. They don't put the needs of others ahead of their own.

- The **Business Goals** program and the right side of the equation require us to live a deliberate life, focusing on what people want most.

- The key component of being relationally conscious is pursuing, pleasing, and meeting the needs of everyone around you, which only happens when you understand and align the needs and expectations of all parties.

POINTS TO PONDER

- Is your job about money and climbing the ladder?

- Are you living in the default mode?

- Are you living life to impress others?

- Until now, how have you measured your own success?

- Have you ever thought about caring more about others than yourself?

- Would you like to live a life with a deliberate purpose and focus—to get what you want most out of life?

6

THE **BUSINESS GOALS** PROGRAM & THE RIGHT SIDE OF THE EQUATION

Todd started his new position in February. The first week was spent setting up his office and getting to know the people within his region. In addition to three months of product-line training, he began the **Business Goals** program and the right side of the equation training through weekly classes held at a local church. He was shocked that this class was held at a church and, frankly, was a little scared by it. He went to the first **Business Goals** class, not sure what to expect.

The class was held each Tuesday morning from 7:00 to 8:00 a.m. A woman named Jennifer greeted him as he walked into the room and introduced herself as the class "Facilitator." She handed each person an overview of the program and a workbook. About ten other people were attending the class. Jennifer started by saying, "Let me explain the **Business Goals** program to you. This is a six-week course. Each class is an hour long and will be interactive. There will be about thirty minutes of video content, and we will have about thirty minutes of discussion. I will connect with you in between classes to discuss the concepts discussed in that week's lesson and how you might implement them in your business or where you work.

As you can see on the card, there are three components to the **Business Goals** program:

Right Goals: An overarching goal is followed by sub-goals required to reach it.

Right People/Right Position: Do we have the right people in the right position to accomplish our goals?

Right Strategy: What must be done to accomplish the goals?

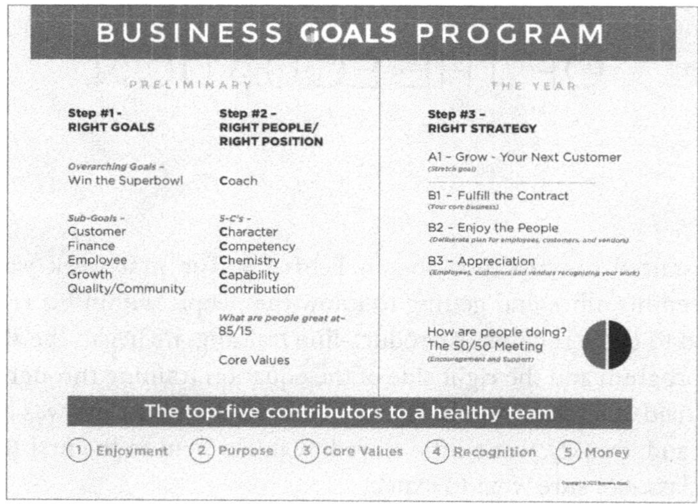

Program Overview

"This card provides an overview of the entire **Business Goals** program. Class graduates often hang the card on the wall of their office or cubicle to remind them of these concepts, sort of as a roadmap for their daily activity," she stated.

It all made sense to Todd. As he went through that first class, he started meeting and interacting with the others in the class. He could see the importance of the material and how Severson had been integrating everything talked about that morning. The class made sense, and he enjoyed the material. He was looking forward to coming back the next week.

Todd drove to his office and pulled in right as Blake got out of his car. As soon as he was within talking distance, Blake asked, "How was your first **Business Goals** class?"

"I liked it!" said Todd. "I can see how so many of the concepts we discussed in the class have been deployed here. I'm looking forward to learning more."

Shaking hands, they walked into the offices. "I'm glad to hear that," said Blake. "It's imperative you understand the importance of the program because it's at the core of everything we do here at Severson. Plus, what you'll learn applies to your personal life as well. I know you have ideas of how you want your personal and professional life to go; we all do. But unless you understand how it's going to work from the **Business Goals** perspective, nothing will come out the way you hope it will," he stated.

"Here's the deal, Todd. When we understand our goals, articulate them, and align expectations with the people around us, especially at home, things change for the better. If you want to be successful in life, you have to deploy the **Business Goals** program and the right side of the equation in everything you do. You'll find that your personal life is where you live the program first. You probably heard them say in class that work is the practice field, and home is the playing field or vice versa. The bottom line is we need to deploy the program in all aspects of our life," said Blake.

> **IF YOU WANT TO BE SUCCESSFUL IN LIFE, YOU MUST WORK ON THE RIGHT SIDE OF THE EQUATION IN EVERYTHING YOU DO.**

Todd had never envisioned learning something at work that he would take home to his family. He needed to think this through. He wasn't sure he wanted to be required to take any initiatives from work home to his family. He was apprehensive about this aspect of his new job but decided to try it for a few weeks.

Blake continued, "You and I will spend the next few months discussing the program and what you learned in each class. First, we'll discuss why we implemented the program and then its three components in greater detail—Step One: Right Goals; Step Two: Right People/Right Position; and Step Three: Right Strategy. But we'll take it further, which I consider the most important part—Step Four: Living It Out. Why don't you get settled and meet me in my office in an hour? The sooner we get you on the right track, the better."

THE THREE MOST IMPORTANT THINGS

In Blake's office, Blake took some time to explain how he had decided the **Business Goals** program was something he believed in and why he made it the focus of how he ran his company and personal life.

"Todd, let's start with some background. I implemented this program out of need. Several years ago, I had two dilemmas in my life that surfaced simultaneously. The first was a problem with my business. I couldn't attract and retain lower-wage earners. They took other jobs for minuscule increases in pay. It was expensive and both mentally and physically exhausting to replace these folks continually. The second dilemma was personal, although it may have been caused by frustration from the first problem. I reached a point where I wondered why I'm here and what I'm supposed to accomplish," Blake confided. "I didn't merely ask myself why I was here at Severson Systems or what I hoped to accomplish in my business; I wondered why I was here on this earth! What did I hope to accomplish in my life? I wanted to understand my purpose, both professionally and personally. As I pondered this question and tried to sort out the problem at work, I realized that the first thing I needed to do was identify what was important to me. Then, perhaps, I could build on my priorities. I spent a considerable amount of time identifying the most important things in my life.

"At the same time, I studied everything I could find on employee retention and motivation. That's when I found the **Business Goals** program. The program creator, Jud Boies, experienced the same employee retention issues in his own company, which caused him to create what is now the **Business Goals** program. He learned that employee retention and what employees wanted most in the workplace had been studied regularly since the 1940s, and similar studies have occurred every few years since then. Every study he found had the same top four or five answers for retaining employees. The number one thing people want in the workplace is to *enjoy the people they work with.* Number two is to *fulfill the contract,* meaning they want to give an hour of their time, talent, skills, and expertise in exchange for a dollar amount. People want to produce something for their earnings. Third is fair treatment—they want to work for a company that is honest, ethical, and serves some purpose for the greater good, a company with strong *core values and is missional in its purpose.* Fourth is *appreciation* or *recognition* for the job they have done, and fifth is *money*—they want to be compensated for doing the job. If they don't get numbers one through three, money becomes number one."

What People Want in the Workplace

1. Enjoy the people they work with, an enjoyable experience
2. Fulfill the contract using their time, talents, skills, and expertise
3. Rules/Core Values that lead to fair treatment
4. Recognition/Appreciation for the job they've done
5. Money/Compensation

"As I read this," said Blake, "it dawned on me that perhaps the solutions to my work problems could also apply to my personal struggles. Boies found that what people wanted in their workplace were the same things they wanted in their personal life, so he created the **Business Goals** program to integrate those things into his own life and the lives of every employee at his company. It worked in his company, and it has worked here at Severson Systems ever since we implemented it."

"That's great," responded Todd. "What did you do to turn things around?"

"Well, as I began to share the process I had gone through to determine what was important in my life, I found that others essentially came up with the same top three. There was a pattern—I was on to something," Blake said, smiling. "Once I found a way to integrate my solution into my professional and personal life, things changed. Every one of our employees started implementing these three priorities into their life. My wife and children did too. It's pretty easy:

1. Identify the three most important things in your life.
2. Integrate them into every aspect of daily living, both professional and personal—via the **Business Goals** program and the right side of the equation."

Todd raised his eyebrows, a smile formed on his lips. "Sounds easy enough. I don't suppose you'll give me any hints about the top three," he teased.

Chuckling, Blake responded, "I don't want to tell you the answers I came up with for the company and myself until you determine your priorities. When you do, I think you will begin to see why you're here at Severson. We'll help you reach your purpose, and you will help us reach ours. Everyone has to know they have a purpose. When you can live it every day, life becomes much more satisfying. The **Business Goals** program will guide your efforts. I've learned that without the disciplines of a program like this, one tends to live in the default mode with no real purpose."

"In other words, you wing it," added Todd.

"Exactly," Blake answered. "So, here's how I want you to identify what's important to you. If you had to name the three most important things in your life, what would they be? It might help by thinking about three different scenarios. First, if you were stranded on a desert island with sufficient food, water, and shelter, what other three things would you choose to have with you on the island? Or say you were on a mission to another planet, and as with the island, the necessities of life have been provided (food, water, shelter). What are three other things you would take? Finally, if you were the last living person on Earth but had plenty of food, water, and shelter, what three things would you choose to have with you? Think of it as three wishes. And choose things that are applicable in all three scenarios. Assume in all three scenarios that you have your health."

THREE HELPFUL TESTS

Blake then introduced the **CAP** test, made up of three smaller "tests," so Todd could weigh whether his possible answers were good ones or not:

CAP Test—Conscience, Announcement, Profit

Conscience Test: A feeling you get inside when you make a big decision. Does it feel right, or does it present that twinge of "something's wrong with it"? We all can decipher right from wrong, and our conscience, if allowed, will usually confirm our decision.

Announcement Test: Can you announce your decision to the world, including your coworkers, friends, and family, and have them applaud you? This assumes you are announcing your decision to people who have moral integrity.

Profit Test: This test evaluates who wins. If all parties involved can win, it's most likely a good decision. But if you win at someone else's expense, it's not a good decision. If someone else wins at your expense, it's not a good decision either.

"The **CAP** test is easy to remember if you can recall what the first letter for each separate test stands for," Blake explained. "They are an offshoot of a more comprehensive test for making big decisions in life that you'll learn in the **Business Goals** class called, 'The Eight Tests for Making Good Decisions.' You'll get to that later. If we run all our decisions through these tests, we will live different and better lives. I want you to make sure your decisions make sense over time. If you were to think ahead a year, five years, or fifty years, can you look back and believe the decisions you made were good ones? If you were on that island for fifty years or on your death bed, would the three things you listed still make sense?"

Todd thought back over his life and some of the things he had done. He quickly realized that many things he had done wouldn't pass the **CAP** test. And they haven't turned out to be good decisions in the long run. He pondered for a second how things might have gone had he known about the **CAP** test.

WHERE DO YOUR DECISIONS STAND WHEN YOU RUN THE CAP TEST ON YOUR OWN LIFE?

Blake encouraged Todd to go home and spend some time thinking about his answers. He also asked Todd to run the same questions by his family. He suggested they determine the three most important things in their lives by evaluating what they would pick in the same scenarios. It would be a good way to have more interaction with them, and he could pass on some good information at the same time. He saw Todd to the door, and they agreed to meet again on Monday to discuss his answers.

That evening, Todd arrived home earlier than usual. Everyone was practically kicked out of the Severson offices by 5:00 and told to go home to their families. For the first week, this felt so strange that Todd had stopped each night at his club for a few drinks, reaching home at his "normal" time between 7:00 and 8:00 p.m. Tonight was different. He was eager to get home and think through his answers about what was important to him.

Sarah and the kids were still out. He was alone in an eerily quiet house. He started a fire, poured a glass of wine, and sat down to consider various solutions. He thought about Blake's different scenarios and the **CAP** test. Would he want to bring some material things like his motorcycle or some of his shotguns for hunting or perhaps his car, clothes, or watch? Golf clubs? As he thought through each one, he began to think how stupid some of them might seem when scrutinized by the Announcement and Profit Tests. Only Todd profited. His conscience almost immediately told him they were not very important things, nor would they make sense over time. From a practical standpoint, there may not be any gas for his motorcycle or paved roads. Clothes might not be necessary for survival. Maybe there would be nothing to shoot, or he would run out of ammunition. The golf clubs would provide little recreation if he didn't have a course. Even if he did, it would be boring to play by himself.

After going over a list of everything he owned or could own, he realized he would be lonely. What he would want most was someone to talk to! He contemplated each of his friends in turn.

Todd thought, *Who would be the best choice?* He spotted a picture of Sarah and his kids on the mantel. He was embarrassed that he hadn't thought of them first. Instantly, he knew his wife had to be his first choice. He thought about their eighteen years of marriage and the many things they had done and been through together. Although they had made many mistakes, he still loved her. They were committed to each other—though perhaps for some of the wrong reasons, like how expensive a divorce would be. Still, he enjoyed her company and continued to find her attractive.

He thought back to the day Anne was born and how close he felt to Sarah and his new baby. It felt good to be a family. He had been so happy with his wife and little girl. He remembered how proud he felt when Scott was born. He thought about all the games they went to with their kids and the many trips he and Sarah took together. They had spent so much time together. As he considered the years ahead, he even thought about death. Who would he want with him as he was dying? An image flashed into his mind—Sarah and the children by his side. They would provide the most comfort and support. And he couldn't leave out his mother, bringing the same comfort she had when he was a child. Yep, no doubt about it. In all the situations that Blake had described—the desert island, the interplanetary journey, being the last person on earth—his family would be one of the three most important things to have. In fact, they were the most important things in his life. What about his closest friends? He listed them at number two. These answers seemed as though they would pass the **CAP** tests as he ran through them, and they made sense over time.

Todd suddenly realized he had spent over an hour contemplating this question. It was probably one of the most profound things he had ever considered. Until he met Blake Severson, he had never felt a need to think about anything like this.

THE FAMILY DEBATES THE QUESTION

As each of his family members arrived home, he asked that they eat dinner together that evening. The kids were mad. It was Friday, and they had plans with their friends. Todd told them to postpone their plans and stick around for dinner. Sarah thought it was unusual but kind of nice.

As they sat down, Todd showed them the program outline and explained each of the three components as Blake had. Though they didn't understand much about the program, they appeared somewhat interested.

Then Todd moved their focus to the most important things question. The kids rolled their eyes, sure that Dad had flipped out. "I'm serious," Todd countered. He described the three settings Blake had mentioned—the desert island, the interplanetary expedition, or being the last living thing on earth. If they were guaranteed all the basics for survival—food, water, and shelter—what three things would be most important to them that would be applicable in such different situations? He asked them to write down their answers and then described the **CAP** test for evaluating those answers.

"What answers popped into your head when I first asked this question?" Todd asked. Scott said he immediately thought of his laptop computer so he could access any information he needed. He thought further and decided he would like some female companionship. He'd bring his girlfriend. Finally, he chose a gun for protection, thinking it would be necessary.

Todd asked him to put his answers through the **CAP** test. Deep down, does a gun makes sense? Could his answers appear in the morning newspaper, and would the readers applaud him? If he were stranded on an island, what good would his laptop do, especially if he couldn't connect to the internet or keep it powered up? Even if he had everything on his hard drive and a solar-powered battery, would everyone profit from him choosing it? Or would he stockpile computer games to satisfy his own interests? The relativity of space and time might make it hard to email friends in a different solar system.

Anne said she'd want to have music. She was sure this would pass the **CAP** test. Surely no one would disapprove of music.

Next, Anne said she'd want her photo albums.

"Why not the people instead of their pictures?" asked Scott.

"Great idea," Anne agreed. "All my friends can come along. And my family—except Scott." She and her brother exchanged sibling sneers. "And third, I'd want a tool kit with a full set of craft supplies—needles, drills, and screwdrivers so I could always be making something. That would be both practical and creative."

"I've only thought of two things," Sarah told them. "What are your three answers, Todd?"

Todd hedged. He didn't want to admit he also had only two answers. A third still eluded him. "I don't want to influence you," he told her. "I'll share my first two now. When you have a third, I'll tell you my third." His first was his family, he said. This included their extended family—siblings, parents, cousins, aunts, uncles, etc. The second was their friends. Both passed the **CAP** test.

"I have the same answers," Sarah said. For third place, she was considering books. She had an extensive library and loved reading. She felt books could pass the **CAP** test. Todd thought books were a great idea. He'd make that his choice, too but included the availability of online books. The family debated their answers for about an hour, the first serious discussion they'd ever had as a family.

When the exchange finally slowed, Anne and Scott suddenly remembered their commitments for the evening and took off, but Todd and Sarah continued talking.

TODD'S FIRST LIST

When Monday came, Todd was eager to tell Blake the answers he came up with. Before he could do so, Blake first explained that Todd's answers would eventually become his personal keys to obtaining and maintaining success and happiness. They are foundational to his reason for deploying the **Business Goals** program in his personal and professional life. If Todd focused on what had the most value for him, and if these things possessed true value, a purposeful and fulfilling life would become inevitable.

Todd made sure he logged Blake's comments in his brain. He sensed this was important to remember. He brought out his list and read it to Blake.

TODD'S MOST IMPORTANT THINGS:

1. Family
2. Friends
3. Books, including online access

Blake expressed pleasant surprise that his first answer was family. Until then, nothing Todd had said or done indicated they were his priority. He asked Todd how he arrived at that decision. Todd described all the scenarios he had considered. None of his possessions mattered on an island, in space, or on his deathbed. He had taken his family for granted in the past, but now, when he thought about dying, he wanted his wife, children, and mother near him. Nothing else could provide the depth of comfort.

Todd described his thought process about his second choice, friends. He was sure this answer could withstand the **CAP** test. And books—he had chosen them after hearing his wife's conclusion, but it made sense. Books could provide information for whatever situation he was in, allow him to continue learning, and offer some recreation.

WHAT ARE YOUR TOP THREE?
USING THE SAME CRITERIA, MAKE YOUR OWN LIST.

"These are good answers," Blake said. "Let's talk about family and friends. Do you remember what I said about the bottom line being less important than everyone winning?"

Yes," said Todd, "but I have to admit that I don't fully understand the concept."

"Then this could be one of the most profound conversations of your life," Blake stated simply. "I believe that relationships with people are one of the two most important things in life. If you do, too, then are you treating them that way? Are you guarding and protecting your relationships with your friends and family? Are you building relationships in your life? We define building relationships as pursuing, pleasing, and meeting the needs of the people around you. It's putting the needs of others first. At Severson Systems, we are intentional about putting the needs of others first by pursuing, pleasing, and meeting the needs of everyone we do business with, including our employees, friends, and family. It's the benchmark of our success."

Todd agreed. "I've seen that already in my business dealings with you. It's what interested me to the point that I am sitting here today."

Blake was delighted. "It is intriguing," he said. "You see, there is no such entity as 'the business' or 'the company'—both are defined by the people in the business or company. People do business with people. Every single thing we do in life revolves around our interaction with others. And success in your life depends on this. You said it yourself—people and personal relationships are the most important things in your life. If you consciously understand this and make it the goal of your life to build relationships by seeking to pursue, please, and meet their needs, you will be successful. I can't stress this enough."

Shifting forward in his seat, Blake zeroed in on the real issue. "Todd, most people focus on the left side of the equation. They are more interested in their goals to acquire and achieve than they are interested in how they interact with the people in the process. This is my impression of you. I believe you have become relationally unconscious. When you interviewed with us, it was all about what you had acquired and achieved, not about the people in your life. It felt like you only had people in your life to show what you had done for yourself. I don't believe you will become truly happy until you figure out how to change your focus to the right side of the equation. When you focus on how people interact to achieve the left side, things will change for the better."

Todd was stunned. Nobody had ever given him feedback that was this direct and biting. Todd's mind drifted for a moment as he pondered what he heard. He knew it was true, but it didn't feel good.

Blake could see his remarks were hitting a nerve in Todd and knew he needed to press forward. "This change in focus requires some changes in everyday thinking. You need to become the same person twenty-four hours a day. You need to treat others in ways that demonstrate you are putting their needs first by pursuing them, pleasing them, and meeting their needs—something few people do. You need to stop excusing negative, hostile, or marginally ethical actions with the phrases 'that's business' or 'I have to look out for number one.' Reject the concept that it is okay to do something professionally that you'd never do in your personal life. There should be no difference between how you act at the office and at home. You should treat your co-workers, customers, and vendors precisely how you treat your friends and family. We must not have one standard for operating at home and a different one for the office. Yet, that is so common in much of the world right now.

"That kind of behavior doesn't build relationships. It's dishonest. It lacks integrity. People take advantage of others, trying to get ahead at other people's expense. They may justify it by saying 'that's just business,' implying it's okay to lie, cheat, or steal in business, but it is not. This tears down relationships because it's selfish. Todd, when you pursue, seek to please, and meet the needs of your family, friends, employees, customers, and vendors, you are building relationships. If you're not doing this, then you're tearing them down. Life doesn't have a neutral position. Anytime people think they're in neutral, they start thinking negatively. There is no mixed message as long as you actively pursue, please, and meet needs. When we get to Step Three in the **Business Goals** program, you will learn how to focus on the right side of the equation in everything you do. That's when things will change in your life."

WHO ARE YOU PURSUING, PLEASING, AND MEETING THE NEEDS OF?

TODD'S OTHER ANSWER

"Now," Blake continued, "I want to discuss your third most important value—books." Blake agreed with Todd's choice but suggested a slight change to a broader category. "Perhaps by books, you mean intellectual stimulation and information. If so, you've come up with the same answers that nearly everyone comes to. Your answers and my answers are similar."

Blake explained that the second most important thing in his life was personal relationships, combining family and friends into a single category. The third was intellectual stimulation and information, keeping his mind busy and fed. "Our brain thinks every waking moment. We can't stop it. It needs to be fed with information constantly. I believe we should consciously choose positive input that pushes us intellectually. Unfortunately, there is a lot of garbage out there to choose from."

Todd nodded in agreement.

"Well done, Todd. I'm not sure you realize the importance of the process you've just gone through. You've been forced to stop and consider what matters the most to you in life—the things you can't live without. When you did this, you determined your purpose for using the **Business Goals** program. Now, what are you going to do with what you've discovered?"

Todd grinned sheepishly as he caught on. "I need to spend my time pursuing them."

"What if you build your life around these things?" Blake challenged. "What if you become deliberate about making sure everything you do feeds this purpose? What if every decision you make is based on how well it supports the most important things in your life? And what if there is a way you could keep these things at the forefront of your mind? I can tell you with conviction that your life will change significantly. It will be more fulfilling. It will bring you true happiness. And your life will provide lasting value."

Blake leaned back in his chair and caught his breath after his impassioned speech. Todd took a breath and leaned back too.

"Todd, if you are continually feeding your brain's desire to learn, building your personal relationships, and living by the rules we all want in our lives, you can't help but be fulfilled," Blake summarized.

Todd was pleased that he had come up with the "right" answers.

Then he realized that his three answers matched only two of Blake's answers. Blake had combined friends and family as his second choice, with intellectual stimulation as number three.

"But what was your first choice?" Todd asked.

"Oh, the first thing on my list is my faith," Blake stated. "Faith, too, shows up on almost everyone's list somehow. Maybe it's hope, purpose, or God. Even though it may be a personal issue to most people, it shows up here at Severson in our rules," Blake smiled. "For now, I want you to concentrate on how the other two principles affect your life and the lives of every employee here. First, we have based our business on building strong personal relationships with each other, our customers, and our vendors by seeking to pursue them, please them, and meet their needs. If this is your personal goal, it is the same as the company's goal. As you go about each day trying to build relationships with customers and vendors, you will be serving one of three things most important to you and helping the company at the same time. We wish more companies would figure it out. It's such a simple equation. But it's difficult to live out, so most people don't do it. They simply don't know how. But the **Business Goals** program shows you how."

Blake said, "The second important thing is intellectual stimulation and information. I work hard to keep new challenges in front of everyone here, from the guy who sweeps the floor to my top vice presidents. When I challenge people with new ideas, new programs, and new goals to achieve, I meet one of their most important needs. In the third step of the **Business Goals** program, you will see exactly how both intellectual stimulation and relationships are at the heart of every one of our staff and one-on-one meetings. But remember, the most important part is the focus on the relationships. Unfortunately, in other companies, they are neglected the most."

It was nearing the end of their time together, and Blake needed to bring the point home. He said, "Now, let's go back to those two dilemmas I had years ago, employees leaving and me wondering why I was here. I said the answers were the same but didn't want to elaborate on them until you had a chance to determine what was important in your life." He handed Todd a paper with the top things he found that employees want to be motivated and happy at work and another paper listing what everyone typically deems as their most important things. "Take a look at these, Todd."

TOP THREE THINGS EMPLOYEES WANT TO BE MOTIVATED AND HAPPY IN THEIR JOBS:

1. Enjoy the people they work with
2. Use their skills and talent to create something of value for the company
3. Rules and Core Values

TOP THREE THINGS ON ALMOST EVERYONE'S LIST OF THE MOST IMPORTANT THINGS IN LIFE:

1. Faith
2. Relationships
3. Intellectual stimulation and information

"Enjoying the people you work with is entirely about relationships. Using your skills and talent to fulfill the contract is entirely about intellectual stimulation. And the rules or core values in our lives are primarily based on Judeo-Christian values dating back to the beginning of recorded time. The rules of our lives are faith-based. Do you see how the answers to both dilemmas converged?" Blake asked.

"That's interesting—I see it," Todd mused.

"The **Business Goals** program became the vehicle that helps us incorporate the three most important things in our personal and professional lives and live them out daily with our employees, our families, our customers, vendors, and friends." Reaching across the desk, Blake grabbed Todd's arm. "Living life with a meaningful purpose is life-changing."

Todd nodded, still deep in his thoughts. *This is life-changing,* thought Todd. And it all made sense. That was the best part.

Blake saw Todd to the door, and they arranged to meet later that week. Blake encouraged Todd to take what he learned home and explain it to his family. Blake never told him this, but one of the reasons he had Todd explain it to his family was that it was a method for him to remember what they had discussed. Once Todd got into the pattern of downloading what he had learned, he kept better notes and formulated the best way to pass it on. It was information that Blake knew his family would benefit from, and it was one more tool to keep Todd engaged with his wife and kids. He was helping Todd enjoy the most important people in his life—his family.

CHAPTER SUMMARY

- People want something more than the obvious.
    - Customers want more than a product.
    - Employees want more than a paycheck.
    - Married couples want more than roommates.
    - Kids want more than a roof over their heads and food on the table.
    - Friends and family want more than just your presence.

- The **Business Goals** program and the right side of the equation help us determine what people want and how to meet their needs.

- When we stop thinking about the wants and needs of the people around us, we become relationally unconscious.

- When we continually strive to understand and meet the needs of the people around us, we are relationally conscious.

- When we are relationally conscious, people around us will help meet our own needs.

POINTS TO PONDER

- Do you want more than just a paycheck at work?

- Do you want something more from your marriage?

- Do you want a deeper relationship with your kids?

- Would you say you are relationally unconscious or relationally conscious?
    - If the latter, what are you doing daily to prove it?

STEP ONE

Right Goals

7

SETTING GOALS AND OBJECTIVES

THE LEFT SIDE OF THE EQUATION

"Todd, the last time we met, we went over the **Business Goals** program's three steps: Right Goals, Right People/Right Place, and Right Strategy. Step One is about establishing a left-side-of-the-equation function, the goals and objectives we want to accomplish," Blake instructed. "We lay the groundwork by setting goals and objectives. Do you have a written set of goals for what you want to accomplish next year?" he asked.

Todd reluctantly shook his head and said, "No, but I have some ideas."

"Don't worry," Blake responded. "I bet you didn't know that only 3% of the population have written goals, and less than 1% update them on a regular basis. I did some research and found some interesting reasons why people don't write down their goals:

1. They aren't serious about their goals.
2. They don't understand the importance of setting goals.
3. They have a fear of rejection or criticism from others about their goals.
4. They have a fear of failure.

"Even worse, studies have shown that only 8% of the people who set goals achieve them.[2] Here's the problem," Blake continued. "Without written goals, our wants and needs change too often, and for many people, that means daily. If you set one goal in your head today and then wake up tomorrow without completing it, you will be disappointed. If our wants and needs change daily, it will be impossible for anyone around us to help us meet our goals because no one knows what we're up to. Remember, in every case, people are required to help us meet our goals. Setting specified, written down goals allows you and those around you to know where you are headed, and they can jump on board. Imagine a company that doesn't have written down goals. Without goals, we wouldn't know if we needed to hire or fire someone. It begins to get absurd. Yet many companies don't set clearly defined goals and objectives and can't convey what needs to be done to their employees. Employees can't read the minds of their managers. They have to know the game plan. And unless employees can fulfill their number two desire in the workplace—fulfill the contract by using their time, talent, and expertise—they won't be happy in their job because they will be frustrated and prevented from enjoying their co-workers."

"I've witnessed this firsthand," Todd agreed, remembering back to his previous job. He now understood why he didn't always enjoy Regent.

"We all have," said Blake. "So, we set very specific goals and objectives, so we know exactly what we are trying to accomplish, who we need to help us accomplish it, and what they need to do to fulfill the contract. We set two kinds of goals—an overarching goal and sub-goals. The overarching goal should be short, concise, and something everyone will remember and be able to restate instantly. The overarching goal instantly reminds us of the big picture and what we are trying to accomplish. The sub-goals are smaller goals that are required to reach the overarching goal. Let's talk about the overarching goal for a few minutes. If we visited any NFL football team in the country and asked anyone associated with the

---

[2] Marcel Schwantes, "Science Says Only 8% of People Actually Achieve Their Goals," Inc.com, https://www.inc.com/marcel-schwantes/science-says-only-8-percent-of-people-actually-achieve-their-goals-here-are-7-things-they-do-differently.html.

team what the goal was for the team that year, we would hear the same thing...." Blake paused, looking for Todd to answer the question.

"To win the Super Bowl," Todd responded.

"Exactly," said Blake. "I believe we would hear the same answer anywhere in America...win the Super Bowl. Even kids as young as ten years old would say that! But it's not that way in most companies. If you walk into most companies and ask anyone what the goal of that company is, you'll get several different answers. In fact, if the company had fifty employees, you might get fifty different answers. How on earth can a company reach any goal if everyone on the team is shooting for a different goal? When we get everyone on the same page, shooting for the same goal, we have a much better chance of reaching that goal.

"At Severson Systems, our overarching goal is to become everyone's favorite company to work with. And when I say anyone, I mean our customers, vendors, employees, and those who interact with us in the community for any reason. We came up with this goal several years ago, and it's become a goal we can really have some fun with. Once we get anyone to admit we are their favorite company to work with, it's fun to ask them whenever we see them, 'We're still your favorite, right?' It gives us both a good laugh, but they also know we are working hard to maintain that favorite status."

Todd thought it was a pretty cool goal and remembered how he was reminded on a regular basis of that goal when his Severson rep called on him at his previous job. He was really glad he had made the move to Severson and liked that everyone was on the same page shooting for the same goal.

"Now that we've looked at Severson's overarching goal, let's talk about our sub-goals. The sub-goals are the incremental goals it takes to reach our overarching goal. And as you will learn in the **Business Goals** class, we use the same five sub-goals they teach in the class." On the whiteboard in his office, Blake wrote down the sub-goals while explaining what each one meant:

1. Customers

"This first sub-goal asks the question, 'What will it take from a customer point of view for us to reach our goal to become the favorite company they've ever worked with?' Since we can't do our business without customers, they naturally come first."

2. Finances

"Finances are very important to every company to stay in business, but there has to be a balance. We ask, 'What will we have to do from a financial point of view to become everyone's favorite company to work with?'"

3. Employees

"To serve our customers at the highest level to be their favorite company to work with, we have to have great employees to help us get there. So the third sub-goal asks, 'What will it take from an employee's point of view to be everyone's favorite company?' If our employees love working here and enjoy the people they work with, that will be conveyed to our customers, vendors, and the general public. Like you learned in the **Business Goals** program if you seek to make the top three things everyone wants out of their job your priority with your employees, it will naturally trickle down to everyone else."

4. Growth

"How will we need to grow to remain the favorite company for everyone? I say this because no one wants to support a company that isn't growing. I believe companies are either growing or declining, and we want always to be growing and getting better."

5. Quality & Community

"And last but not least, we believe that we have a responsibility to set an example in our physical community and our industry. One of the best ways to set that example is by selling the highest quality products in our industry. When we strive for the highest quality, our employees feel great about our company and what they represent. We don't believe we can be anyone's favorite if we aren't considered the best quality in the industry with the best customer service and delivery."

"So these are the five sub-goals we put in place at Severson, and we have measurable metrics attached to each one of them," Blake said. "We use the **Business Goals** app, which you've seen, to track our progress toward these goals through daily, weekly, monthly, quarterly, and annual goals." The app was one of the first things Todd was shown how to log into on his first day at Severson. Blake asked Todd to pull out his cell phone and pull up the app. Since Todd was familiar with the app from the **Business Goals** class, he went right to the Goals page. It showed the overarching goal and the five sub-goals they had just discussed.

Business Goals App

"Todd, one of the key components to our goal-setting is that they are easy to understand. When you get an entire company focused on one set of goals and get each person to understand their contribution to those goals, you have a good chance of succeeding. In the people-side of the equation, you will see these goals help every person become a contributing member."

SETTING INDIVIDUAL GOALS

"In the **Business Goals** class, you learn the program applies to your personal life and professional life. I'm encouraging you to apply it in both areas. This is important because you won't be able to reach the goals you set at work if things aren't going well at home. People think they can compartmentalize and separate what's going on at home from work and vice-versa. But it's not possible. If you have a rough period at work, it will take a toll at home. You will begin to exhibit poor behavior with your wife and kids. The opposite is true as well. If you are having a rough time at home and things aren't going well with your wife and kids, you will begin to exhibit poor behavior at work. Get things going great at work and home, and watch how things start improving. You will be energized in both places."

"As you might have guessed," said Blake, "it will be very important for you to set your individual goals as they relate to the company's corporate goals. It's essentially your contribution that will help us achieve our corporate goal. What are the four or five things you need to accomplish this year so the company can reach its goals? As a regional sales manager, you play a vital role in the company's overall sales. Your region represents 14% of the company's overall sales, so it should be fairly easy for you to determine your number one goal. I want you to develop your top three to four goals over the next few days as part one of your homework assignment."

"Done," promised Todd.

"So, for part two of your homework assignment, I want you to determine the goals and objectives for your family for the following year. I know you said you have ideas of what you'd like to accomplish in your head, but I think it will be very important to write them down. I also want you to follow the same methods we use here at the office. Create an overarching goal for your family and then sub-goals. For your sub-goals, you might want to consider these categories:

1. **A goal for just you and your wife.** Maybe you can describe ways you want to grow deeper in your marriage and how to spend more time together.

2. **A financial goal for the year**. Describe what it might look like if you manage your money the way the best money managers in the country prescribe to.

3. **A goal for your kids.** Perhaps a plan about what you want to teach them this year as they prepare to be on their own.

4. **A goal for how the family will grow.** Try asking and answering how your family could grow and learn over the next year.

5. **A goal for your family as part of our community.** This may be something like making a goal to be a model to other families; how to contribute to our community through community services or serving somewhere that helps our community.

"Todd, when families have written goals like this, things run differently. You told me your folks divorced when you were in middle school. What do you think would've happened if they'd had this exact set of goals in writing and did their best to achieve them? There is a good chance they may not have gotten a divorce because they focused on meeting each other's needs. Now go develop a set of written goals for your family and then written goals for your job," Blake encouraged, escorting Todd to the door.

TODD'S FAMILY SETS PERSONAL GOALS

Todd went home and called for another family dinner night. At dinner, he explained what he had learned and wanted the family to develop a set of goals for the year. What did they want to accomplish in terms of their marriage and the kids? Todd's family initially thought it was a waste of time, but Todd brought up Blake's comment about his parents and how they may not have gotten a divorce when he was a kid if they had set goals annually. The family agreed and spent some time talking about their goals. Todd and Sarah set one of their goals to grow closer to each other in their marriage. They set a goal to be better parents even though neither of them could define what that might look like. They also put some financial goals and a goal to take at least three family vacations that year. They were off to a good start.

CHAPTER SUMMARY

- Approximately 3% of the population has written goals.
- Of that 3%, approximately 1% update those goals regularly.
- Only 8% of people who set written goals achieve their goals. The other 92% stay stuck or float along in life.
- We need both an overarching goal and several sub-goals to meet the overarching goal.
- You need to write down goals in all aspects of your life:
    - Personal
    - Work
    - Family

POINTS TO PONDER

- Do you have written goals?
    - If not, why not?
    - What has prevented you from writing your goals down?
- What would you like your overarching goal to be?
- What sub-goals do you need to reach your overarching goal?

STEP TWO

Right People/ Right Positions

8

PUTTING PEOPLE WHERE THEY DO BEST

THE RIGHT SIDE OF THE EQUATION

"The following week, Todd arrived at Blake's office at his usual time, ready to discuss the next step in the program. "Come on in," Blake offered, smiling as Todd entered his office. "I can't wait to talk to you about the next step of the **Business Goals** program. We have a lot of ground to cover, but first, how did you do on your company goals, and then how did things go with your family?"

Todd took a seat. "Good! It went well on both assignments. I spent some time looking over our corporate goals and figured out what my personal contribution to those goals might be," he said, handing Blake a piece of paper that spelled out five sub-goals for his work:

1. $64 million in sales for the region
2. $9.8 million in net profit for the region
3. 21 new customers (15% growth for the region)
4. Fully-trained backup for each member of my team (including me)
5. 100% customer satisfaction (with 1% return rate)

"My region represents 14% of the company's revenue. I looked at our corporate financial goals and figured out what 14% of those goals were," he explained.

Very good, Blake thought. He was pleased to know Todd gets it. "This is perfect, Todd. Just what I was looking for," Blake encouraged. "Now that you understand Step One, let's look at the dynamics of how people play into those goals. You can't possibly reach your goals without people. We've learned that we have a much better chance of meeting the company's goals if we also understand our employees' goals. If you'll remember, we talked about that in our first meeting. People want to enjoy the people they work with, they want to fulfill the contract by using their skills and talents to accomplish something for the company, they want rules to follow that make sense and tie into their core values, and they want to be recognized for the work they complete. I like what Jim Collins had to say in his book Good to Great, that to have a successful team, we need to 'have the right people in the right seat on the bus,'"[3] Blake said. "For Severson Systems, it's imperative to make sure everyone here is serving in the best position for them—the right people in the right positions. To determine this, I ask two simple questions:

1. Can you support and defend why each person is on your team?
2. Are they more valuable to you here, or would you rather have them working for your competitor?

"The first question should be answered with the help of three tests: the Windfall Test, the 5Cs, and the 85/15 Test. The second question is fascinating because in an instant, you have to look at everything a person brings to the table, both good and bad, and decide if you want to have them on your team and if they'll help you win your 'Super Bowl,'" Blake told Todd.

---

[3] Jim Collins, *Good to Great: Why Some Companies Make the Leap and Others Don't* (New York City: Harper Business, 2001).

"These questions are asked and answered all the time in professional sports. Players are traded between teams, and some may not play very well on one team, only to be traded and do great on another team. I believe this same concept takes place in the workplace. People will join our team for a little while or a long time. Some will flourish here; others will glean something from our team, serve their purpose at Severson, and get released to serve somewhere else. From time to time, we will also have some disruptors who would be much better off disrupting someone else's team instead of ours. As a manager, continually ask and answer these questions for everyone on your team, 'Can you support and defend why they are on your team and are better playing on your team or for a competitor?' Do that, and you will always have the right people in the right seat," Blake concluded.

"I mentioned there are three tests to help you make those decisions. Let's start with the Windfall Test, and I'll guide you through what can help you with your team members."

9

THE WINDFALL TEST

"Todd, I think the Windfall Test from the **Business Goals** program is brilliant because it is simple to administer. In a matter of seconds, it provides you with a simple screening test to see if you have someone in the right seat on the bus. At least it provides an initial indicator for what people are skilled at doing, and even more importantly, what they want to do." Blake handed Todd a piece of paper explaining the ground rules for the Windfall Test.

"Ask your employees (or anyone) how they would spend their time if they had all the money they ever needed to live. Start by giving them some ground rules like these:"

WINDFALL TEST—GROUND RULES

1. They came into a "windfall" of money of some kind, like a very large inheritance or they won the lottery or their stocks went through the roof. They have all the money they could spend.
2. They spent two years doing everything they had ever dreamed of doing. In other words, they completed their bucket list.
3. They purchased all the home, cars, boats, and toys they ever dreamed of owning. They have it all.
4. Now they were bored and need something to do with their time.

What would they do? How would they spend their time?

Blake thought it was important for Todd to know the origins of the Windfall Test from the **Business Goals** class, so he said, "The idea for this test came from a large physicians group. The hospitals the doctors were contracted with were complaining because patient scores were very low. It turns out doctors and nurses weren't getting along, and because of this, patients had poor experiences. Knowing what you know from the **Business Goals** class, you should understand that the doctors and nurses were not enjoying the people they were working with. You'll see why in a moment. Every doctor was asked what they would do if they suddenly came into a windfall of money. The good news is that 95% of the doctors said they probably wouldn't be able to wait thirty days before wanting to 'pull a shift' in the hospital. They hadn't gone through twenty years of schooling to sit on a beach somewhere. They enjoyed healing people and making them feel better. But the other 5% said they would leave their jobs so fast heads would spin. Who do you think was responsible for why people didn't enjoy who they were working with? The 5% who didn't want to be there. Once those discontented doctors were helped 'off the bus,' everything turned around.

"It's quite simple, really," continued Blake. "By asking people how they would spend their time if they didn't need to earn a living, we can find out what they enjoy doing. People enjoy doing things that utilize their natural skills, expertise, and experience. Even people in repetitive or seemingly mundane jobs will often say they would still do something that utilized their ability to do those mundane tasks. So when you deploy the Windfall Test, you will get an initial indicator of whether the person is close to being in the right position or not.

"I also love to ask the Windfall Test question as an ice breaker when I meet people socially. It's easy to ask and gets people talking about their favorite thing to talk about—themselves. You can learn a lot about the person, and you can instantly know if they are potentially in the right seat where they work or if they might be stuck and unhappy," Blake told Todd.

This all made sense to Todd; it was an interesting concept. He was already thinking about using it as an ice breaker, and he would use it with his wife and kids too. He loved that idea.

"Todd, may I ask what your answer to the Windfall Test was when you were asked it in the **Business Goals** class?" Blake asked.

"Sure," said Todd. "Since I have always loved cars and interacting with people, I would probably find a nonprofit or someplace to volunteer that uses some of the same skills I use in my current job. I mean, why not? People need help with cars, right? I can't imagine not ever working with cars. I would miss it."

That's exactly the answer Blake was hoping for. Todd would be doing something related to the auto industry using the same skills he used every day in his job. It proved, at least initially, that Todd was in the right seat on the Severson bus.

CHAPTER SUMMARY

- Asking people how they would spend their time after doing everything they've ever wanted to do provides a good indicator of whether they are in a job that utilizes their skills, expertise, and experience.

- Even people in repetitive or mundane jobs desire to utilize the abilities they've been given to do those kinds of tasks…and enjoy it.

- If people describe spending their time doing something completely different in terms of job skills and expertise, they may be in the wrong position.

POINTS TO PONDER

- How would you spend your time if you encountered a windfall and never needed to worry about money again?

- Based on your answer, are you utilizing your skills, expertise, and experience in your current role?

10

THE 5CS

"There is another test I want to discuss a few minutes that will help you discover whether you have the right people in the right position—the 5Cs you learned in the **Business Goals** program," Blake told Todd. "We use the 5Cs Test when evaluating our team and when we interview any potential new hires. In fact, we used the 5Cs when we interviewed you; you just didn't know it. The better we get at detecting where people stand relating to the 5Cs, the better the teams we build. Remember that the 5Cs all represent attributes we look for in people to determine if they will be a good fit on the team."

"Yes, there are five of them—character, competency, chemistry, capability, and contribution," replied Todd.

"Great! Yes. Let's talk about character first, and then we'll get into the rest. We value all of these attributes highly here at Severson."

CHARACTER

"We believe a person's character is determined by how well they live out the rules we all want to live by. Now, people tend to set their own relative bar for morality; seldom do they use an absolute bar. The absolute bar means there is one immovable standard. The relative bar allows people to adjust their standard based on the current situation or collective society.

Most people use relative rules and ethics," Blake explained.

"Here at Severson, we strive for an absolute set of rules that we've all developed. But it's not easy. We all make mistakes regularly. But we strive for it because those we do business with expect nothing less. Everyone we do business with wants us to live up to those rules we have in place. When we don't, they lose trust, which will affect their decision to do business with us. However, this also is relative. Though people expect us to be moral and ethical, they are surprised when we are because society has allowed us to break the rules as a common practice. We want to raise the bar back up to the absolute level for two reasons: 1) it's the right thing to do, and 2) it will set us apart from everyone else. Make sense? Are you following me?" Blake asked.

Todd was overwhelmed by this explanation. How could he ever be perfect? "I'm not completely sure about absolute and relative rules—could you explain that more?" he asked tentatively.

"Sure, happy to," said Blake. "Let's see. If we were to take honesty as a rule we are evaluating, we could measure whether a person was 100% honest in every situation or if they were mostly honest or only somewhat honest. If we were to ask the average person if they were honest, they would likely say 'yes,' and it would be a relative answer. They would do a quick evaluation and determine that compared to most people, they were honest. But if we pressed a little harder, we could find out if they were absolutely honest or relatively honest. We could ask them if they ever embellish or withhold information. Do they ever round up numbers or add a little extra information in stories to make them sound better? Do they report 100% of their income or try to squeeze in a few questionable deductions? Do they always tell their boss the truth or withhold information? How about in a sales situation—is everything disclosed when a person asks a specific question? Do they tell what they would consider a white lie, meaning it was harmless because no one would be hurt by it?

"For those who we're around a lot, we can watch, listen, and know whether they're honest or not. If we can't gain personal experience, then we have to either ask people close to them or ask them questions that might help us determine their character. We want to do our best to find prospective employees who desire to strive for the absolute bar. We encourage our employees to do their best to live up to our rules. We all want to do our best to live up to our standards," Blake clarified.

"So, Todd, when you interview someone, there are two questions to ask. First, do they believe that for us to be successful in business, we need to be slightly more honest than our competitors (i.e., the relative bar), or do we need to strive for the absolute bar? Second, when you show them the rules we've put in place, do they have a desire to live up to those standards at the highest level? Based on past performance, would this be difficult?"

Todd shifted in his chair. Absolutes weren't his strong suit.

COMPETENCY

"Moving on to competency, it is the sum of the pieces that comprise a person's skills. We ask, 'Does this person have the mental and physical ability and perhaps the experience necessary to do the job?' To answer this question, we look at the person's track record, education, and experience, then compare that to the specific requirements for the position. If there are two areas that managers tend to underhire in, they're competency and capability. Many companies think that if they hire a less-experienced person to do the job, they can pay less and train them up into the position. It seldom works. Too much time is lost training because they're not competent in that position.

"We've learned this the hard way. When we were young and growing, we needed a new production manager. We hired someone who scored really high in the character, chemistry, and capability areas but lacked experience and, consequently, was less competent. As a result, he didn't contribute much, and we struggled. When we recognized how important competency was and we made an investment in the right person, we were so surprised at how different things were. We thought we over-hired for the position with our next production manager, who did the same thing at a much larger company. It worked. Hiring someone with more experience than we thought we needed turned out great. Part of what attracted him to the position was the growth opportunity he saw in our company. But the biggest attraction was our rules. We are a company of integrity, which was more important to him than a firm of relative ethics," Blake explained.

"We've learned our lesson, and now we only look at people who appear to be overqualified for the position and are clearly competent. Take you, for example. I'm guessing you thought you could do this job in your sleep."

"That is true," Todd acknowledged.

"We did our homework. We knew exactly how much you could generate, and when we moved you in to your region, we nearly doubled our expectations for that region based on where we placed your competency level. We believe that competency is a significant component of being able to contribute. Todd, remember this. Look for a person two levels above the position you're trying to fill. Even if it costs more," Blake advised strongly.

CHEMISTRY

"Now, let's talk about chemistry," Blake continued. "This one is sometimes difficult when recruiting and interviewing people because they will naturally put their best foot forward. Often it's not until you spend more time with them that you can better assess the chemistry. That's why for any significant hire, we always include a lunch or dinner in the interview process. If the person is married, we do all we can to get their spouse to the lunch or dinner. We like to watch how the person interacts with their spouse. How do they treat them? What is their interaction like?"

"We glean a lot of information that way," Blake continued. "It also plays into their character. You may think that was absent from your interview process, but we had already had several dinners with you and

Sarah on some of our promotion trips. We had a good feeling about the chemistry component with you. But with people you meet for the first time, you need to get away from the office and spend time in everyday life to get to know them. The bottom line question we ask ourselves about any hire is, 'Can we invite them to our home for dinner, again and again, and enjoy it?' We try to form an opinion on everyone, even our part-time employees. It's an excellent indicator of whether we like someone or not. Remember, it's the sum of the pieces we look for in a person, not any single attribute."

CAPABILITY

"Capability is sometimes hard to evaluate, and the one I believe is overlooked the most. We want to find the answer to the question, 'Is there anything going on in the person's life that would prevent them from operating to the best of their ability?' Is there a significant change in financial condition, like a bankruptcy? Is there a change in their marital status or family status? Are they just coming out of rehab? We can't legally ask that question directly. What's more, the average person would answer no. Most people think they can overcome the seasons in their lives and continue to perform to the best of their ability. Statistics and experience reveal something very different. Good season or bad, both will take a toll on performance in the workplace and their personal life.

"For the new hire, we are looking for the beginning or recent end to a major event. We look for changes in family status, such as recent marriages or divorces, deaths or serious illnesses, recent births, and even children recently leaving the house for college. Because many of these questions are personal in nature, we need to be very careful, so we don't break any laws. This is another good reason for going out to lunch or dinner because people will often relax and start talking about what's going on in their lives. They might give us a clue as to whether they are in the midst of a season or about to go into or come out of one. We can ask very simple questions about what the person does for fun and what a typical weekend over the past month looked like.

"If a person had a recent change in the family, that will likely come up as they describe recent weekends. Once they bring it up, you can usually ask them other related questions. For example, if the person says she usually spends weekends with her husband and children, you can ask how long they've been married and the age of the children. If you hear they've been married for two months, but the kids are twelve, ten, eight, six, and five, you know you likely have someone who was recently remarried and now has a blended family. Blending families can be complicated in the early months, and this person is likely in the midst of a season that is both good and bad. Their performance probably won't be at its best for at least six to twelve months. This may be okay, but we need to plan for it—we need to know what to expect and how to help them with that process. We want them to be an outstanding member of the team once the season is over," Blake asserted.

"We also need to recognize that when we relocate an employee for a position, their performance will not be at its peak for some time because we are putting them through a season. Starting a new job is a season unto itself. We all know there's a ramp-up period. When we move entire families into a new community, we have to expect that they will be going through some change that will impact their ability to function at work and at home for several months. We need to recognize this and help people through those seasons. One of the best things we've done is to make sure we don't try to kill the person with production in the first few months. They need to be at home early and make sure their family gets acclimated. We want to make sure they have a really good balance for the first three to six months on the job," Blake explained.

CONTRIBUTION

"Finally, I want to talk about the final 'C'—contribution. We can get someone who has all the character, competency, chemistry, and capability we're looking for, but if they can't or won't contribute for some reason, they cannot be a viable part of our team. Let me explain.

"For the new hires, the contribution component must be based on their track record. Have they already had a good scoring career? That's the question we're looking to answer. Professional baseball and basketball are good analogies to use here. If one team is looking to pick up a free agent, they will look at most of the 5Cs and see if there's a fit with their team. For the contribution component, they look at their ability to put points on the board. In baseball, they look at the batting average. In basketball, they look at scoring, rebounding, and assists. Many teams will think some improvement can be made with great coaching. However, they will not take players with sub-par scoring ability and hope to change them dramatically. The same is true in business. You cannot take someone who tells you they will be a big contributor to your team but has never been able to do it before. They may give you great reasons for why they couldn't do it in the past, but you shouldn't make the deal without a track record. We've learned this the hard way, too. We've had many people pass the first four Cs with flying colors, but they had a horrible scoring career. We've learned that these people are good talkers and can sell you what they think they can do, but they've never actually done it before.

"For your existing team, it's usually something different. Sometimes a person has had a good career and has been able to contribute but is beginning to falter. When this happens, it's usually one of a few things. Either the person is in the midst of a season, and it hasn't been recognized, or the job demands have changed, and you've outgrown his competency level. Or perhaps the person is simply tired of pushing the performance requirements and wants to slow down. The problem with the latter is that many employees often feel entitled to remain in a position they've done for so many years. They forget they were paid the wage they agreed to for that performance, and it didn't entitle them to an extended payout while they didn't do anything. Sometimes you need to write that down, so the employee recognizes they are being paid for this month's work, not a payout over many years," Blake explained, looking somewhat perturbed.

"Todd, the 5Cs are an essential component to success in business. They are the key to having the right person in the right position on your team so they can score the most points. Remember these when you deal with your existing team so you can diagnose problems and use them when you are evaluating someone new for your team. As usual, keep these in mind at home. You're not going to get rid of any of your family members, but you can diagnose problems that may be a result of a weakness in one of the 5Cs and then help them work through the issues."

Blake pulled out his cell phone and brought up the **Business Goals** app, adding, "We use the **Business Goals** app to keep track of the 5Cs for everyone here at Severson Systems. This very simple, objective scoring system gives us a quick snapshot of each person. You'll want to keep track of every person on your team relating to their 5Cs with the app." He showed Todd the button to find the 5Cs and then walked him through the scoring system.

Business Goals App

TWO OTHER CS

"One last thing I want to mention is something from the **Business Goals** class—the other two Cs they discussed. The first one was coach, and this one applies to you. When we supervise other people, we are their coaches. The primary job of a coach is to encourage and support their players. To do that, we need to understand where they are in each of the three tests we are discussing today. When we see they are a little low in any area, our job is to 'coach them up' in that area. If someone scores an 80% in contribution, our job, as their coach, is to try to bring them up to a 90% in that area," said Blake. "You'll find that when you take a baseline evaluation of everyone on your team for the 5Cs and then work with each person on your team to improve their scores, three things will happen:

1. Their morale will be boosted. Most people like being coached to improve in each of the 5Cs, plus this helps us achieve the goal to enjoy the people we work with.
2. Overall team performance improves. When we improve in the 5Cs, we get along better and make more significant contributions to the team and the company. This adds to the goal to fulfill the contract.
3. They will live up to the rules of your organization. Improving your character often means living with more integrity and playing more according to the rules. This satisfies the goal of working for an ethical company."

"The other C stands for caustic," Blake said. "Every once in a while, we will come across someone who is caustic. They are unhappy, and we cannot do anything that can change it. We've learned that caustic people just need to be released. Whenever we release a caustic person, we hope they land in a place that is a better fit for them where they can thrive. Life is too short to live every day unhappy."

Todd couldn't agree more.

CHAPTER SUMMARY

- A person's character is measured by how well they live out the absolute rules of our society, not relative rules.
- Most people would say they are honest. But that might mean slightly more honest than most other people than 100% honest.
- Competency is the sum of a person's skills.

- It's best to hire someone with more competency than less for a position.
  — When in doubt, overhire.
- The best test for chemistry is, "Can you invite the person over for dinner and enjoy it, again and again?" If possible, include their spouse.
- Capability means, "Is there anything going on in the person's life that would prevent them from accomplishing their goals?"
- If a person is going through a season, don't overload them with work. Do the opposite.
- Contribution is a person's ability to accomplish what they were hired for, "putting points on the board."
- Beware of those who talk a good talk but have accomplished little.
- Your role is to be a great coach by encouraging and supporting those on your team to be the best they can be.
- Some people are "caustic," and the only thing you can do with caustic people is to release them and hope they do better on someone else's team.

POINTS TO PONDER

- Would you say that you are 100% honest, mostly honest, or slightly honest?
- In what areas are you very competent?
- How would the people around you pass the chemistry test?
- How would you pass the character test?
- Is there anything going on in your life that's affecting your capability on the job?
- Can you put points on the board (contribute)...both at home and work?

11

THE 85/15 TEST

"We have a little bit of time left, so let's finish our time today talking about the third test from the **Business Goals** class, the 85/15 Test. I think this is also a brilliant test because it is collaborative in nature, fun, and affirming to everyone when we go through it. It's usually very accurate," said Blake.

"We deploy the 85/15 Test exactly how the **Business Goals** program prescribes. Our teams get together in a room based on who works the closest together. Most of our team are groups of twenty-five or less, which is perfect. More than that, and people don't really get to know each other. We then ask one person to grab a cup of coffee so we can do their 85/15. We ask everyone in the room to first make a list of everything great about the person getting the coffee. What do they do really well that we wouldn't want them to stop doing? What are their greatest strengths for the team? What are their greatest skills, attributes, and characteristics? What do we want them to do more of? We give everyone just two minutes to make their list. Then we ask them if there's anything the teammate doesn't do so great that we should have them stop doing. We ask them to make that list in one minute," Blake explained.

"Then we use a whiteboard or poster-sized sticky note and go around the room asking each person to give us just one of the things on their list—the positives first. We keep going around the room until we have everyone's contributions to the list. We then make a second list of the things the person doesn't do so well, again going around the room with each person giving us just one of the things on their list. I'm always so surprised, and I know I shouldn't be, that the list always comes out almost exactly how the **Business Goals** class explained. About 85% to 90% of the overall list is positive about the person, and about 10% to 15% of the list is negative.

"When we bring the person we just evaluated back into the room, their expression is nearly always the same, 'yep, that's me…no surprises.' Everyone looks forward to the 85/15 Test because it's an affirming process. People love hearing how other people view them and what they do well. It also shows us the strengths of our team and potential deficiencies. We can see where we need to add talent and where we need to coach our players up.

"In a few circumstances, we learned we've had people in the wrong seat on the bus because of what comes out in the 85/15 Test. It's not that they were terrible people; we just weren't utilizing their natural skills and abilities because of the role we had them in. When we moved them to a different role that used those talents brought out in the 85/15 Test…they flourished.

"We've also learned, just as the **Business Goals** class explained, that the 15% side of the test is very important. We have to make a choice when looking at their 15% list. Is the item on the list an integral part of their job, or can we simply take it off their plate? If it's an integral part of their job, we have to coach them up in that area. If it's not, we have to take it off their plate.

"This is crucial because often people will spend a lot of time working on something on their 15% side that no matter how hard they work they will never produce a good result. They might spend 50% of their time working on something only to deliver a poor result, which results in overall failure in their position. When we remove it from their plate and allow them to focus on the things they do great, we often see double the contribution from the person. Not only that, they are happier, more enjoyable to work with, and they put more points on the board.

"Using my NBA basketball team as an example, a player might have scored low on his ability to make free throws. That is an important and integral part of the game that can't be removed from any player's job description. The player would have to be coached up in that area. Similarly, the same player might be exceptional at layups but poor at dribbling the ball. The coach can easily have someone else move the ball down the court (dribbling) and then pass the ball to the player we're discussing to make a layup.

"Todd, when we run the 85/15 Test, we get a snapshot of what everyone is great at on our team and where we need to coach them up. When we know what each person excels at, we can better place them so they always produce great results and are happy doing it. When everyone on the team is performing according to their strengths, the overall team excels, and we almost always reach our goals," Blake said.

Todd nodded. He could see clearly how the 85/15 Test could help things. He had never really thought about any of this before the **Business Goals** class as a way to build others up and handle employee shortfalls. It was something he wanted to experience firsthand. "I've heard of 360 evaluations before. Did you ever use the 360 before the 85/15 Test?" he asked.

"Yes, before we learned about the 85/15 Test and **Business Goals,** we used to run 360 evaluations," Blake answered. "It sounds like you're familiar with that, but it's where people above, below, and beside a teammate on the org chart would evaluate them. We never really had a great outcome because people wouldn't always look for the best in their co-workers. Just by virtue of the 85/15 title, we evaluate people's strengths and, by extension, play to their strengths. It has become a much more positive and affirming evaluation process for our team. Because of that, we try to run the test at least once a year, sometimes twice.

"Before you go, Todd, I just want to leave you with one other thing. When you met Sarah and started dating, you began to determine the great things you liked about her. There were probably some things you weren't thrilled about, but the great things overshadowed the ones you weren't thrilled about. Those great things were so strong that you chose to ask her to marry you. She did the same thing with you. Sometimes in marriages, we change our gaze to the 10% to 15% side of the equation and choose to live there. This becomes destructive and often leads to the demise of the marriage. At Severson, we choose to look at the positive in people and build them up in those positive characteristics and attributes. I would encourage you to think about the 85/15 Test at home and choose to live in the 85% ... don't let the little things that aren't so great consume your thoughts about your wife. I bring this up because, just as the **Business Goals** class taught us, we need to be the same people twenty-four hours a day. When we deploy the concepts of the **Business Goals** course in all aspects of our life, especially our marriage, it always goes better. I hope this makes sense," Blake told Todd.

"It does make sense," said Todd. "You know, at first, I thought it was weird that you told me much of what I would learn when I joined your company would apply to my personal life. I had never heard such a thing. But after trying each of the things you've told me to take home, I can see the importance. It's been great. Thank you for spending this time with me each week."

Blake was really pleased with the way Todd was embracing the **Business Goals** program. He felt Todd was a great addition to Severson Systems and was looking forward to seeing him grow both professionally and personally.

CHAPTER SUMMARY

- The 85/15 Test shows our teammates' strengths and weaknesses.
- 85% to 90% of most people have good, positive attributes...we need to remember that and focus on those.
- Everyone has 10% to 15% of their makeup that isn't great or

composed of things we don't do well, but we don't have to live in that 10% to 15%.

- Consider focusing on the 85% that's positive in the people in your personal life...it will pay big dividends.

POINTS TO PONDER

- Is it a general practice at your company to focus on the 85% to 90% great things that people do?
- Do you have people on your team defined by their 15%?
- Consider taking the things people don't do well that aren't an integral part of their job off their plate completely.
- Only coach up those things that can't be removed from someone's job and can't be given to someone else, but expect it still may not improve to perfection.

STEP THREE

Right Strategy

THE FUTURE

12

DEVELOP AND POST RULES AND CORE VALUES

Blake and Todd met the following week. Blake began the meeting by introducing Step Three, which puts the right strategies to meet the goals.

"There are many parts to our strategy of becoming everyone's favorite company to work for and with. It's one thing to have goals and objectives and the right people in the right positions to carry them out, but now we get down to tactics—the various things we do to get there. As you learned from the **Business Goals** class, rules and core values are the third most important thing people want in the workplace and at home. My experience is that most people follow a very loose set of rules, often making them up as they go or adapting them to the situation. But even though most people don't live by a set of absolutes, they expect others to. We talked about this in our last meeting. You expect people to be 100% honest with you, but I'll bet that you are not 100% honest. If you're like most people, you may tell them what you think they want to hear, even if it's not entirely accurate. Am I right?" Blake challenged.

Todd somewhat agreed. He wasn't willing to admit that Blake was right, but many memories of this very thing instantly came to mind.

"Here at Severson Systems, we believe you need to follow an

absolute set of rules or core values, both in business and personal life. We know that our rules are important in meeting others' needs, and to be effective in a relationship, we must follow these rules. I can tell you that our standards are pretty high, but I know they are what you want in your own life too. We've also learned that most people want everyone to adhere to the same rules. I use a simple little exercise to prove this. If you were to move to a new town, what characteristics and attributes would you look for in your new circle of friends? Here, write this down," said Blake, handing Todd paper and a pen. "Make a quick list of the ten to fifteen attributes that come to mind."

Todd started writing a list, the answers coming easily.

HONEST

AUTHENTIC

MORAL

GIVING

CARING

SINCERE

HELPFUL

POSITIVE

FUN

RESPECTFUL

EMPATHETIC

INTEGRITY

DEPENDABLE

AVAILABLE

STRAIGHT PRIORITIES

Blake looked over the list and smiled. "This list is almost identical to the list we use here at Severson Systems. I've asked this question of every employee here and have kept a running list of the answers. I have about the same fifteen terms. These are the criteria that folks use for choosing their friends. It's also the rules they want to live by and expect others to live by. Isn't it interesting that everyone has the same general criteria? This means that we all should be able to be friends. The only missing component, of course, is chemistry. The point is that we all have a set of rules we want our friends to live by, and they hope we live by them too. Though my experience is that not everyone will live by a set of rules unless we are made aware of them, discuss them, and hold each other accountable to them regularly, so, at Severson, we post our rules of conduct throughout the company so everyone can be reminded what they are," Blake explained.

"We like how the **Business Goals** class has taken all the rules or core values they had ever heard of and condensed them into ten basic core values. We've adopted these core values as the rules we want to live by here," Blake said, pointing to a picture on his wall that lists all ten rules:

BUSINESS GOALS CORE VALUES

Priorities
Highest value = highest priority

Accurate Representation
Look at the whole, not a distortion.

Integrity
Do what's right and truthful with civility.

Balance
Balance your time wisely between work, family, faith, hobbies, and self.

Leadership/Teamwork
Add value to all situations and people.

Respect
Recognize each person's value.

Self-control
Use your mind and body appropriately and honorably.

Prosperity
Strive to gain on your own, not at the expense of others.

Honesty
Be 100% honest, not 99.9%.

Contentment
Understand your limitations.

"I can tell you that it's highly likely that every problem you've had in your life violated one of these principles. Conversely, when you live by these principles, I think you'll find things go pretty well. Life gets simpler. As a company, we want to live by the same attributes and high standards that we want as individuals," said Blake.

"Todd, the rules we live by play a vital role in what's important to us in life. You stated that family and friends were two of the three most important things in your life. We expect our family and friends to live by the same rules we value. Unfortunately, very few have a written list of these rules to live by, nor do they discuss them unless they're violated. When you have a printed code of conduct, can see them regularly, and discuss them with each other, they become easier to live by. That's why we post them in our offices, in the bathrooms, in our conference rooms, and on our website and social media pages. We want everyone we work with to know we live by these rules and invite them to hold us accountable. It's part of our strategy to be the company everyone loves."

Todd understood how having the rules and core values stated, posted, and discussed would make a difference. It was simple and made sense. More pieces to the puzzle were falling into place.

Blake continued. "Since we are deliberate and passionate about the **Business Goals** program, I want to make sure you understand these 'rules of conduct.' Let's spend some time going over these behaviors, so you'll know exactly what they mean to us. Severson employees know these rules in detail and refer to them regularly. I can tell you from experience that it's delightful to work at a place where everyone understands the rules and their meaning. It's so simple, yet no company I've encountered has defined its rules and incorporated them into their daily activity the way we have.

"This practice has another benefit. It allows us to deploy our policy manual regularly. This may not sound like much, but it's very significant. We use a large national labor law firm to counsel us and ensure we follow state and federal laws. When they saw the rules and how we deployed them, they became very interested. Our attorney, Larry Sebastian, told us that employers repeatedly have the same problem when an employee brings a suit against them. The first question a plaintiff's attorney will ask is, 'Is there a policy in place?' Let's say the issue is sexual harassment. Every employer would answer in the affirmative. The next question would be, 'How do you deploy this policy?' If we were asked that question, we would state that we have a policy and that it's deployed through our bi-weekly training program. We discuss the rules of our company and encompass every item in our policy manual, including sexual harassment. We show the training dates, the participants, and the topics discussed. We have a plan that allows an employee to express concern over any policy, state or federal law, or moral issue in an anonymous manner. One attorney told us that this program might be the only logical defense an employer has."

Todd was impressed. And, once again, the time had flown by. As Todd left, Blake encouraged him to go home and introduce the rules and core values to his family. "Run them through the same drill and see if they come up with the same answers. After all, the same rules apply in your home, right?" asked Blake.

Back in his office, Todd studied the rules of the company that were framed on his wall. The idea that rules are no different in your home is an unusual concept. The more Todd thought about it, the more he realized it was true. If his family lived up to the rules, they would logically get along better. As Blake had stated, it had something to do with being relationally conscious and playing into everyone's ability to enjoy the people they live, work, and do business with. By making some simple changes in terms, he could present the exact same rules of conduct to his family.

HOMEWORK: PRACTICE THE RULES

That evening, Todd asked his family about the criteria for choosing friends in a new location. They quickly concluded that Todd was being transferred and began offering reasons why they couldn't possibly move. Only when Todd guaranteed that this was a hypothetical exercise could they calm down enough to answer the question. Sure enough, they came up with a very similar list as Todd's.

Todd showed his family the rules that Severson had posted on their website; then, they made a list of the ones his family came up with to put on the refrigerator so everyone could see them. Todd was anxious to see what impact these written rules might have on the Hanson household.

The following Friday, Todd shared with Blake how the "rules" evening had gone. He mentioned he put his family's rules on their refrigerator. Blake was very pleased with how far Todd had taken their lesson. He went out of his way to call in a few of the other staff members and company vice presidents and praised Todd for what he had done. They had a simple celebration, which really made an impression on Todd. He walked on air for the next three days.

CHAPTER SUMMARY

- There are rules in society that we expect each other to abide by.
- Often, we expect others to follow the rules to a greater extent than we do ourselves.
- The ten basic rules we all want to live by are:
  - — Straight Priorities
  - — Accurate Representations
  - — Integrity and Civility
  - — Balance
  - — Leadership/Teamwork
  - — Respect
  - — Self-control
  - — Prosperity
  - — Honesty
  - — Contentment
- Your rules have a direct correlation to your company policies. The **Business Goals** program will help you deploy your company policies regularly.
- Developing and living up to rules in your life is a component of being relationally conscious and a requirement to enjoy the people around you.
- It's not difficult to make a list of the rules you want in your life and post that list in frequented areas around work or home.

POINTS TO PONDER

- What rules do you expect people around you to follow?
- Do you follow the same set of rules?
- Who holds you accountable for following those rules?
- Are your rules absolute or relative to the situation?
- Do you need to follow the rules only a little better than the next person?
- How might people behave around you if you raised the bar and followed absolute rules?

13

FULFILL THE CONTRACT

THE LEFT SIDE OF THE EQUATION

The following week, Blake was excited to meet with Todd because they would cover the final two sessions of the **Business Goals** program…what they call the "secret sauce." There are two parts to it: fulfilling the contract and enjoying the people you work with. These are the top two things everyone wants at work and home. Most people are only aware of fulfilling the contract. That's the left side of the equation. Enjoying the people you work with is the right side of the equation, and when people put equal effort into both sides of the equation, they become wildly successful.

Blake and Todd met at their regular time. Blake jumped right in, "You'll remember from the **Business Goals** class, the final two meetings show how to fulfill the contract from everyone's perspective, which is the second-most important thing everyone wants. And then we learned how to make sure everyone enjoys the experience—the number one thing everyone wants. Deploying the right strategy is about making sure we understand both of these concepts, so let's talk about fulfilling the contract this week. Fulfilling the contract is about meeting people's expectations. We all have expectations in nearly every situation. The problem is that everyone is always guessing at those expectations instead of simply asking what the expectations are. This is true in the workplace and at home. Your wife has expectations of you, but I'll bet you don't know what they are, and

I can prove it. Do you have a list from Sarah of the four or five things that would make you her dream husband?" Blake asked.

Todd laughed, shaking his head no.

"No problem—most people don't have that list. But tonight, when you go home, I want you to ask your wife to write out a list of the four or five things you could do that would make you her dream husband. Let me tell you what happened when I did this the first time. I went home one evening and asked my wife, Mary, for a list of the ten things that would make me her dream husband. Her first response was, 'What are you after?' as if I had an ulterior motive. I did have an ulterior motive. I had just completed this part of Step Three in the **Business Goals** program, where I learned how important it was to pursue, please, and meet the needs of people around me to fulfill the contract. I followed their direction to start at home with my wife, seeking to pursue her, please her, and meet her needs. But as I thought about it, I realized I wasn't sure what her needs were, so I thought I'd just ask her. I explained that to her, and she agreed to make a list. A few days later, she handed me her list. I was relieved to find it didn't have anything I couldn't do. She listed things like, 'tell me you still love me; tell me I'm attractive to you; be a good provider for the family, and other things like that.' So, I did my best to incorporate some of those things into my daily activity for the next few weeks. Later, I asked her how it was going, knowing it must be pretty good if I was incorporating the list into my daily activity. I was surprised when she appeared disappointed by my efforts. 'Well, things are a little better,' she said.

"I was dumbfounded! 'What do you mean?'" I asked.

"She said, 'Well, you are sort of doing eight, nine, and ten on the list, and they are only worth about half a percent each, so things are one-and-a-half percent better.' A light bulb went on above my head. The list had priorities, and the items were weighted. So I asked her to take the list back, put it in priority order, and attach a weight to each item. A few days later, I received the list again but in priority order with weights. The first item was worth 50%, and the second was worth 40%. If I did the first two items on the list, I'd be golden, I thought. So for the next few weeks, I made sure to incorporate number one and number two on the list. So how do you think things went for me?"

"Much better, I suppose?" Todd guessed.

"Yes! In fact, things went from good to great. We had a good marriage, but when I started working on the most important things to her, many things changed for the better. It was great! What do you think that list is called?" Blake asked. Before Todd could answer, Blake blurted, "Job Description for Spouse!"

"Here's the problem," said Blake. "We think we know what our spouse wants from us because we've been married for a while, but we're only guessing. And because we're not mind-readers, we usually guess wrong. The same thing happens at work. Our employees think they know what we want them to work on, but they will guess unless we are clear. So we need clearly defined job descriptions. The moment I recognized the list my wife gave me as a job description for a spouse, I realized the same thing was true with my children and at work. They all had expectations of me and me of them. Within a week, we were crafting new job descriptions in the office. Not the kind that states very high-level generalities and ends up in the bottom drawer of your desk. I'm talking about a specific list of what the person needs to do to be our dream employee. And that list must be specific, prioritized, and weighted. Let me give you a real-life example of what happened."

FIRE THE ACCOUNTING DEPARTMENT

"When I asked my wife to give me her list, I was struggling in the office with a few departments. I was ready to fire the entire accounting department. They just didn't get it, and it seemed like they couldn't do anything right. Then I asked them to write their job descriptions using the same method I had used at home: make a list of the three or four things you do in the office daily, put it in priority order, and give each item a weight. As soon as I received the CFO's list, I instantly saw the problem. The number one priority on his list was Accounts Receivable, which he gave a weight of 40%. He reasoned that if he didn't collect the money for the company, we might not be in business long. Second on his list was Accounts Payable, with a weight of 30%. He reasoned that we might not be in business long unless he paid our vendors. The third was Purchasing Systems, with a weight of 20%. He reasoned that because we had so many people with purchasing power, he needed to make sure systems were in place to make sure the purchasing was done properly and with the right constraints. The fourth was Reporting, with a weight of 10%. He reasoned that he needed to provide me with reports regularly so I could make decisions.

"When I saw the list, I thought, 'No wonder I want to fire them. The list is in exactly the reverse order and with the reverse weights!' I explained to him that he needed to get me accurate reports on a timely basis so that I could make decisions. This was the most important thing to me, with a 40% to 50% weight. My second was the purchasing system. We had many people who could buy things on behalf of the company, and I wanted to make sure we had some controls to keep them from buying things they shouldn't. This was easily worth 30% to 40% to me. The third was Payables. We had always paid our vendors on time. It was probably worth only 10% to me. The last thing on my list was the Receivables. We had contracts with everyone we sold to with tight controls on when they paid. Everyone we sold to paid us like clockwork. It only needed to be looked at once in a while by the accounting department to make sure it was on track. Again, this was only worth about 10% to me.

"When they clearly understood what I wanted, in what order, and how heavily each item was weighted, they changed how they did things to meet the needs on my list. The weight told them how much importance and, therefore, how much time should be spent on each item, and the priority told them the order to work on things. It was very simple for them to change how they worked on things, and once they were delivering what I wanted in the right order, things changed dramatically. They became one of the best performing departments here, and I didn't fire one employee," said Blake.

"That's incredible, Blake! What a difference!" Todd exclaimed.

"Look, the bottom line is that part of our strategy needs to be about prioritizing what we work on every day, so we are working on the top three to five most important things with the highest priority and weight. These become prioritized tasks. But there's a small problem. There might be twenty or thirty tasks you could attempt on any given day. So, you have to get with your team and your supervisor, run your list by them, and make sure everyone is on the same page about the priorities."

Todd really appreciated this story and already knew the changes he wanted to make with his team. What a simple concept but so profound and helpful! He was excited.

Blake said, "I loved how the **Business Goals** program explained and graphically showed this. They gave an example that is so true when they asked, 'Have you ever walked by someone's desk and wondered, 'Why in the heck are they working on that?' They wanted to fulfill the contract but didn't know what to work on, so they picked what was the most fun or easiest for them. You'll remember this picture from the **Business Goals** class."

	Bob	Sally	Joe	Mike	Phil	Steph	Amanda
1		X					
2				X			
3	X						
4			X			X	
5							
6							
7	X						
8						X	
9				X			
10	X				X		
11	X				X		
12		X					
13							
14						X	
15		X	X				X
25				X		X	X
40			X		X		X

Pointing to a graphic in the workbook, Blake said, "The left column represents the priority level of the thing the person is working on. You can see that Bob is working on the third, seventh, tenth, and eleventh most important things he could be working on. Amanda is working on the fifteenth, twenty-fifth, and fortieth most important things she could be working on. If we were to put weights on each item, we know fifteenth, twenty-fifth, and fortieth wouldn't score much of a percentage of importance. These people want to fulfill the contract at work, but without knowing the most important things, they will work on what's most fun and easiest for them. I was working on eight, nine, and ten on my wife's list because they were the most fun and easiest for me to accomplish, but they were only worth a half a percent each to her," Blake explained.

"Our goal is to get everyone working on the top three to four things, by priority and weight attached to our company's goals, departments, and ultimately the individual. When that happens, we almost always reach our goal. You'll remember what that picture looked like from the **Business Goals** class," said Blake, pointing to the next graphic from his workbook.

	Bob	Sally	Joe	Mike	Phil	Steph	Amanda
1	X	X	X	X	X	X	X
2	X	X	X	X	X	X	X
3	X	X	X	X	X	X	
4	X		X	X	X		
5		X					
6							X
7						X	
8							
9							
10							
11							
12							
13							
14							
15							
25							
40							

“This is what we strive for here at Severson Systems. Everyone knows the most important things to work on, by priority and weight, and seeks to accomplish those things each week. And as you’ve seen, we use the **Business Goals** app to track this,” said Blake, again showing Todd where this was on the **Business Goals** app on his phone.

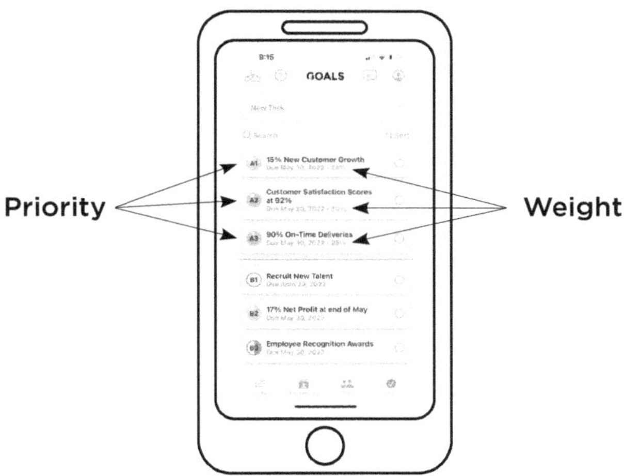

TIE THE TOP THREE OR FOUR PRIORITIES TO THE GOALS

Todd had heard everything that Blake had just explained in the **Business Goals** class, and it made sense to him, but it became so much clearer when he saw how it was being put into action in real life at Severson. But Blake wanted to make sure Todd understood another key part of the strategy in accomplishing the overarching goal and sub-goals: tie the top three to four priorities on our task list to our goals.

“Todd, in the **Business Goals** class, you were introduced to a concept called the ‘Above the Line’ and ‘Below the Line’ goals. If you recall, the concept took the top four priorities and separated them into two categories—Above and Below the Line. The line simply represents a distinction between two types of goals. The Above the Line goal is a goal that brings growth and energy to a company. It’s the company’s lifeblood as new customers and growth keep the company moving in a positive direction. Without new growth, companies stagnate and die a slow death. At Severson, our Above the Line goal is our growth goal. It's defined by the percentage of growth we are striving for and measured by annual sales. If you go to the **Business Goals** app, you'll see that you can define any new task as an Above or Below the Line task/goal, and you can see what goal it's tied to." Blake pulled up the app on his phone and showed the page to Todd.

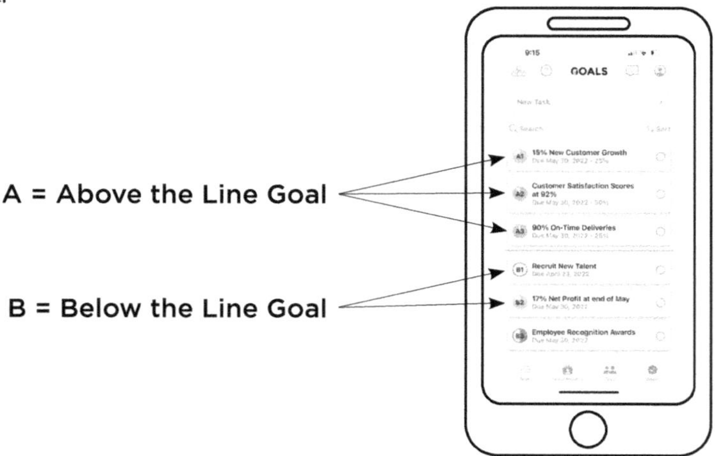

"The Below the Line goals are what we must achieve to stay in business. They consist of fulfilling the contract with our customers, including things like delivering products on time at the right price and of the highest quality in the market. Other Below the Line goals are tied to fulfilling the contract with our employees by meeting with them each week and aligning expectations. A third goal is tied to being deliberate about creating a good experience for everyone who encounters Severson Systems. When the top three or four prioritized tasks we do every day are tied to our overarching goal and our sub-goals, that's when we make significant progress. This strategy has been at the root of our continued success ever since we implemented the **Business Goals** program."

Blake began to escort Todd toward the door and remembered he had one more thing to add. "Todd, there's one last thing that's perhaps the most important thing I can tell you today. Remember that the second most important thing everyone wants, including our employees, customers, vendors, and family, is to fulfill the contract. It applies to your family as well. I went to my wife and asked her for the list to fulfill the contract in my marriage with her, and I did that by seeking to pursue her, please her, and meet her needs. Can you imagine what happens when we seek to do that with everyone around us? When we seek to pursue, please, and meet the needs of our customers instead of our own, everything changes, and we can become their favorite company to work with because we are putting their needs ahead of ours. My marriage went from good to great because I put my wife's needs ahead of mine. She then wanted to find out what my needs were so she could meet them by priority and weight, and now my needs were being met. When you combine this with the second part of the **Business Goals** 'secret sauce,' I think you'll see why it all works and how we've been so successful."

As they walked out, Blake encouraged Todd to go home and get the list from his wife of the four to five things that would make Todd her dream husband. He agreed to ask Sarah for the list that night.

CHAPTER SUMMARY

- We have expectations for the people around us, at work and home, which must be communicated because nobody can read minds.
- Expectations have to be discussed regularly—weekly is good.
- Since we all have needs, why not just develop a list? Our list of expectations should be prioritized and weighted.
- We have expectations of all the relationships in our life—personal and professional.
- There are usually twenty to thirty things we could be working on at any given moment.
- Without a priority system, you will naturally choose what's more fun or interesting to you.

- The top three or four most important tasks worked on each day should be put in priority order, weighted, and tied to the company goals.
  - — An individual's goals would support a department's goals.
  - — A department's goals would support the organization's goals.
- Above the Line goals bring growth, energy, and excitement to a company.
- Below the Line goals keep the doors open by meeting the needs of your existing customers, your employees, your vendors, and your family too.
- You should create goals for work, family, and yourself.
- Use the **Business Goals** app to track your goals, progress, and the goals of everyone on your team.

POINTS TO PONDER

- Do you have a list of the four or five things your spouse, children, and boss want from you to become successful in that position?
- Have you ever thought about the weight and priority of the things you work on?
- Have you considered that your customers, vendors, and family have a top three to four prioritized tasks you could be doing to meet their expectations?
- Are your personal goals tied to your department's goals?
- Do your goals have measurable milestones to track and achieve?

14

CREATE AN ENJOYABLE EXPERIENCE

THE RIGHT SIDE OF THE EQUATION

"Hey Todd, have a seat. It's time to talk about a critical part of the strategy that aligns with the right side of the equation. It's another part of Step Three in the **Business Goals** class and is considered the most part because it addresses the number one thing people want at work and home: to enjoy the people in their lives. And to do that, you have to understand how to create an enjoyable experience," Blake told Todd.

"Before I learned about the **Business Goals** program, I thought the number one goal of my company was to make money. Because of that, I spent every waking hour trying to figure out how to be more profitable. I think most companies have a similar focus. Yet it doesn't address what people want most: to enjoy the experience. Think about this for a moment. Would you rather do business with a company whose primary goal was to first have a great experience with them and then fulfill the contract based on meeting your top three to four most important things? Or would you rather do business with a company solely focused on its bottom line?" asked Blake.

"Well, when you think about it that way, it's almost comical. Nobody would want to do business with a company solely focused on making a profit," Todd exclaimed. "I know I wouldn't."

"You're right," said Blake. "I learned the same thing was true at home. My family didn't want me to just provide for them financially. They wanted me to spend time with them and for it to be an enjoyable experience. They wanted to enjoy being with each other and do things as a family. When I asked my wife for a list of things that would make me her dream husband, they contained things that were much more than providing for her financially. Most of them pointed to things that enhanced our experience with each other."

"So let's talk about creating an enjoyable experience for people. It's about being interested in their lives, doing life with each other, and taking an interest in what interests them. We pursue them, try to please them, and work to meet their needs in all aspects of life—it's not just about how they perform. You have to get good at relationships and understand that people value their relationships above everything else. The number one thing on everyone's list—'enjoying the people'—is about having great relationships with everyone, including our customers, vendors, employees, and family members. We will become everyone's favorite company if we build the best relationships with them, meaning a better relationship than they have with any other company," Blake explained passionately.

"I want to give you a few examples to show you the difference it makes when you focus on the right side of the equation. You had told me that Severson was one of your favorite companies to work with before you joined us. What were your reasons for that?" Blake asked.

Todd thought about it a minute and concluded that he really had enjoyed meeting with his Severson rep every time they met. In fact, he was his favorite rep to meet with. When he thought about why, it was because his rep always took an interest in Todd's life. He knew Todd's hobbies and interests, his family, his friends, what was going well in Todd's life, and what wasn't going so well. They had become friends because of how much the rep knew about Todd. His rep had taken an interest in Todd's life and always found a way for Todd to talk about what he was most excited about or most concerned about. Todd had formed a lifelong relationship with him, and they did a lot of business with Severson as a result of it. His rep knew how to engage in the right side of the equation and did it every time they met.

Todd explained everything he had thought about to Blake. He could see that the right side of the equation played a significant role in how much work his previous company did with Severson Systems and why he had become such good friends with his Severson rep.

Then Blake brought up his second example. "Todd, when you think about buying any products or services, I'll bet you base your decision on the right side of the equation without even knowing it. Let me prove it. Let's say you and Sarah are going out to dinner. You have three places in mind, and all three are about the same distance from your house. They are also about the same price, and the food quality is about the same, so which one do you choose? My bet is you'll choose the one where you will have the best experience based on the level of service, how the staff interacts with you, and where you will have the best time. It's those interactions that matter most. If the restaurant knows your name and recognizes you as a regular customer, and goes out of their way to treat you as if you are friends with them, that's the place you will go. Am I right?" asked Blake.

Todd agreed. He had never thought about it before, but it was true.

"And when companies are deliberate about creating that experience, they are more successful. But it has to be genuine. So many companies have heard that it's important to create an experience but fabricate it and mess it up. When that happens, it's a disaster. I hate it when I walk into a store, and someone yells at me from across the store, 'Welcome in!' They try to be friendly and form a relationship in five seconds, but it's not genuine. You have to build and earn relationships. They don't happen because you force them into existence," Blake told Todd. "There's a very specific way to build relationships that will form true and lasting relationships instead of phony ones. I'd like you to focus on how you can create an enjoyable experience with your team, customers, vendors, and family—every time you get together, just like your former Severson rep did with you."

CHAPTER SUMMARY

- The **Business Goals** program uses a specific, proven method for building relationships.
- The number one goal in your company should be to build relationships, not make money.
    - If you focus on building the relationship, the profit will naturally follow.
- Enjoying the people you work with is entirely about your relationship with them. They value relationships with others above everything else.
- Building relationships requires you to be relationally conscious—to focus on the needs of others by pursuing, pleasing, and meeting their needs.
- When you take an interest in what interests them and engage in the right side of the equation every time you are together, the other person feels valued, and a relationship forms.
- Companies that are intentional about building genuine relationships are the most successful.

POINTS TO PONDER

- Do you believe building lasting, genuine relationships is more important than money?
- Has your focus been on building the bottom line instead of building relationships—with your customers, vendors, employees, and family?
- Can you see how focusing on making every aspect of working with you an enjoyable experience could become the most important thing you do?

15

IDENTIFY AND UNDERSTAND YOUR ROLES

Now Blake knew he needed to cover a major component about roles. What did Todd believe was his role? Not just at Severson, but with his family, community, and life. It was sure to be a great discussion.

"Ok, so to create an enjoyable experience for the people in your life, how well you play your roles with them is key. I believe each of us is in one of three different roles throughout the day and throughout our lives:

- Mentor (leader, father, supervisor, coach, teacher)
- Peer (friend, coworker, spouse)
- Student (child, employee, volunteer)

"It's important to identify and understand the roles you are in and how others perceive you in these roles. Whether we like it or not, people expect different things from us in each position. One role you take on during the day is that of leader. You might be a supervisor, coach, father, or mentor. The second role is that of a peer—you might be a coworker or friend, and this applies to your spouse. The third could be a student or someone being mentored. That's the role you are in right this minute, Todd. If you think about it, you move in and out of these roles all day long. You're a father when you get home, a boss within your department, a coworker or peer during sales meetings, and a student at other times—like now. Once you identify the role you're in, you need to understand what is expected of you. What are your duties and responsibilities? Most importantly, what do the people you interact with need from you? What do they expect of you? Let me ask you a question, Todd. Do you have a desire to be a great parent to your kids?"

"Of course, I do," Todd replied.

"Well, what does a great dad look like? What attributes does he have?"

Todd pondered this. "Well, he is a good leader. He is encouraging, fair, patient, loving, comforting when necessary, a teacher, and has good communication skills."

"Exactly right. In fact, we've worked up a list over the years of the attributes of the perfect father, adding to it from time to time. It's the same list I use for the perfect mentor, supervisor, and coach. Here's a copy. It includes the characteristics you just mentioned and a few more. Tell me if you agree with the others."

The Perfect Mentor/Coach

Honest
Moral
Authentic
High level of integrity
Respected
Visionary
Positive
Friendly
Empowering
Sensible
Comforting
Teaching

Personable
Rewarding
Disciplining
Encouraging
Experienced
Communicative
Courageous
Driven
Patient
Intelligent
Fair
Respected

Caring
Focused
Humble
Forgiving
Recognizes my skills
Empathetic
Supportive
Strategic
Reasonable
Brings out the best in me

"Do you see anything on the list you don't agree with or would like to take off?" Blake asked.

"No, I like all these attributes," Todd told him.

"Do people think you are all of those things when you are in the role of supervisor, coach, mentor, or father?"

"I hope so, but probably not," replied Todd.

"You're probably right. But, since you have a desire to become that person, we're going to do our best to help you get there. This is another strategy we use to get to our goals, and I think if you dig into this concept, you'll see the difference it can make in your relationships. Let me give you the lists we've developed over the years for the Peer/Friend role and Student role. See if you see some similarities on the pages," said Blake, handing Todd two more sheets of paper.

Perfect Peer/Friend List

Honest
Moral
Authentic
High level of integrity
Friendly
Respected
Responsible
Objective
Sincere
Comforting
Accessible
Committed

Encouraging
Straightforward
High level of integrity
Loyal
Candid
A good listener
Confidential
Constructive
Caring
Kind
Trustworthy
Empathetic

Considerate
Open
Shares in your pain
Shares in your gains
There for you
Supportive
Sets a good example
Non-judgmental
Has similar interests

Perfect Student List

Honest	Dependable	Open minded
Enthusiastic	Punctual	Willing to learn
Interested	Respectful	Attentive
Authentic	Consistent	Does not procrastinate
Positive	Grateful	Non-judgmental
Respected	Helpful	Has good study habits
Mature	Committed	
Courteous	A good listener	

"Todd, if you knew this is what people expected of you when you were in one of these roles, and you did your best to be that person, can you see how things might change? How would this contribute to building relationships? These characteristics and attributes are essential for others to enjoy the people they work with. Every employee here at Severson has a copy of these three lists. Part of our regular staff meetings and one-on-one meetings is to go through the lists and make sure we're living up to them. We hold each other accountable to the lists. I encourage every employee here and my family at home to tell me when I'm demonstrating something other than the characteristics on the list. Allowing others to give me this kind of feedback holds me accountable and helps me build stronger relationships. I don't just allow people to give me feedback, I seek it. But don't worry that it might allow some people to take advantage of me. Nothing will change the fact that I am the boss here. I own the company and will remain the person who makes the final decision until I replace myself, sell the company, or die. The same thing holds true of you as a parent, coach, or mentor."

It all made sense to Todd. He was all ears.

SEEKING FEEDBACK IS KEY

"So once we understand the roles we play, we begin to tackle how to get better in each of them. One way to do this is to seek feedback from the people in our life. We are intentional about seeking feedback to see where to improve. People respond to feedback in three different ways. Some people are closed to feedback—they don't want it, and they won't accept feedback from anyone. Others are open to feedback if asked whether they want some feedback. The third are the people who seek feedback. Todd, you'll find that the most successful people in the world are the ones who seek feedback in everything they do. The most successful athletes continually seek feedback from their coaches on how they can improve. The most successful politicians seek it after every speech. Here at Severson, we meet every week to discuss how we did the week before. We are intentional about seeking feedback to see where to improve."

HOMEWORK: RECOGNIZE YOUR ROLES

"Now. Todd, I want you to start critiquing your role as father and supervisor, husband and friend, and student. I'd like you to seek feedback in each one of those areas from the people you interact with. Rate yourself for every attribute on these lists and ask people to give you feedback on items from the lists too. Then strive to improve where you need improvement. We actually score each other on how well we do in each of the roles as part of our scorecards. I'll tell you more about that later," Blake concluded.

After their meeting, Todd started observing the people in his office, noticing how they carried out their various roles. All seemed to strive to demonstrate the qualities on the three lists. He found the responses and reactions they were getting from co-workers most intriguing. Everyone was asking for feedback on so many different topics. This process caused people to have more respect for each other, and people were more polite and had a positive and friendly attitude.

Later at home, Todd studied the qualities of a mentor and tried to improve himself in areas where he had often failed. He'd never been very patient or encouraging with his kids. This was his biggest challenge. He made a point of giving each of them some support every day. He started small, so it didn't come off as patronizing. Scott and Anne had a little more bounce in their step within a few days and showed him more respect.

He also planned to ask each of them for feedback after a month of being deliberate about being a better dad.

CHAPTER SUMMARY

- There are three roles we move in and out of each day:
    - Mentor (leader, parent, supervisor, coach, teacher)
    - Peer (friend, coworker, spouse)
    - Student (child, employee, volunteer)
- If we can identify the roles we play and improve on them, we can create an enjoyable experience and move toward our goals.
- People who meet their goals make a habit of seeking feedback from others to improve in their roles.

POINTS TO PONDER

- What roles do you play in each category, and to whom?
- Looking at the attributes for each category, how well do you rate yourself? Where do you need to improve?
- How would others rate you in those roles?

16

IMPLEMENT THE 50/50 MEETING

THE SECRET SAUCEW

Blake knew this week's meeting with Todd would be a big one. The concept of the 50/50 Meeting is where the left and the right sides of the equation are deployed and brought into balance. It's the "secret sauce" to the whole program, and they had a lot to cover.

"Okay," Blake began, "let's talk about how we deploy the secret weapon of the **Business Goals** program where everything comes together—the 50/50 Meeting. Just like they recommended in class, we use the 50/50 Meeting here at Severson all the time. This concept is fundamental, Todd, and I believe that if you practice it regularly, you will be significantly more successful in your personal and professional life. It's that life-changing. There are two kinds of 50/50 Meetings. One is with a group, and the other is a one-on-one meeting. Different things are accomplished at each meeting. The group meeting is designed to celebrate the great things our teams are doing and allow other teams to communicate anything they may need to tell each other. The one-on-one is designed to align personal expectations with your supervisor to determine if you can do anything to help them succeed in their role and position. The key to the 50/50 Meeting is spending the first 50% of the time discussing the left side of the equation—a person's goals, objectives, and how to be successful in their position—fulfilling the contract. The other 50% is spent on the right side of the equation—building lasting and meaningful relationships with the people," Blake explained.

"The order of things is very important. We discuss the goals and expectations first, then finish with what's going on in the lives of the people at the meeting. Here's why. The first part of the meeting explains what we need to do to succeed in our role and fulfill the contract. People want to know they are fulfilling the contract by accomplishing something significant for the company using their time, talent, and expertise. The second half of the meeting gets down to enjoying the people they work with. If you first show them how to be successful, then spend the right amount of time talking with them about whatever they want to talk about, they will leave the meeting energized. They will leave knowing, consciously or subconsciously, 'My boss told me exactly how I can be successful in my role, and he was interested in me as a person.' This is very different from how I used to run things," Blake confessed.

"Remember how I told you this program first started? I had trouble attracting and retaining employees and learned the most important thing they wanted was to enjoy the people they worked with. Well, it started with me. They didn't enjoy me. It was because I appeared to have a one-track mind and focused strictly on business. When I walked through the building, I was so focused on getting the job done that I didn't even recognize them as people. I didn't smile much, I didn't talk to them much, and I didn't do anything that recognized them as anything other than an employee who was there to get a job done.

"As I started to have meetings with them and actually talked to them as people, they told me more about their lives and vice versa. We started relationships that didn't exist before. I did care about them; I just didn't know how to show them I cared. My method of acting like I cared was to ask how the family was as I walked them out of my office or back to their work area. I was the boss who focused 98% on getting the job done and 2% on how they were doing as employees. If I were to pursue them, try to please them, and do my best to meet their needs, I would have to spend more time with them to understand what those needs were. Boy, was I surprised at the outcome! As we deployed the 50/50 Meeting, it was easier than I expected, but the most shocking thing was the result. I enjoyed my employees, and they enjoyed me! When that happened, our turnover rate dropped dramatically, and productivity went up. My employees didn't want to let me down by leaving or underperforming. Everything improved. And it was so simple.

"Over the course of the past several years, we've developed and refined the 50/50 Meeting. In this process, we've found it applies to our employees, customers, vendors, and people in our personal lives. It's the key to being relationally conscious. If you spend as much time truly talking with them as you do telling them what to do, you can't help but form a relationship. And you never have to discuss anything personal if they don't want to," Blake explained.

Todd understood what he learned about the 50/50 Meetings in the **Business Goals** class, but it made more sense when Blake explained how they lived it out at Severson. He was ready to delve more into each one.

CHAPTER SUMMARY

- The 50/50 Meeting is one of the essential tools of the **Business Goals** program that balances the left and right sides of the equation—the secret sauce to making the whole program work.

- There are two types of 50/50 Meetings:
  - — Individual: Aligns personal expectations with the supervisor and identifies areas where they need help;
  - — Group: Celebrates accomplishments and allows for communication between departments.

- The key to a 50/50 Meeting is to:
  - — Spend the first 50% of the meeting aligning expectations and fulfilling the contract;

  - Spend the second 50% of the meeting talking with the person as a person, enjoying the people you work with.

POINTS TO PONDER

- How might you start holding 50/50 Meetings with the people around you?
  - At work?
  - At home?

17

THE GROUP 50/50 MEETING

"Now that you know the basics of the 50/50 Meeting, I want to teach you how we live them out here at Severson. We'll start with the group meeting. At Severson, we have two types of group meetings. We have the all-staff meeting in which the entire company gets together. We try to do this weekly but never less than every other week. The other type of group meeting is our department meeting," said Blake.

"In our all-staff meetings, the goal is celebration and communication. We spend the first half of the meeting celebrating any great accomplishments from the week before. We ask people to report anything that happened, or someone did that deserves celebration by department. Then we talk about the things going on this week, ending with anything special someone should know about what's coming up next week. I like to spend a fair chunk of the time telling the team how we are doing as a company and giving them something uplifting or encouraging about our future, or maybe talk about some topic important to the company's DNA. Sometimes we talk about what's going on in the world and how we play into those things either as individuals or as a company. These meetings are designed to be encouraging and uplifting. We want to celebrate publicly and correct privately," Blake explained.

> ***We celebrate publicly and correct privately.***

Continuing, Blake said, "Our department meetings are designed to get more into the details of the teams and get work done. We spend half of the meeting informing each other about goals and accomplishments and seeing if anyone needs anything from anyone else to accomplish what they need to. We take care of companywide directives and go over individual goals that the team needs to hear. But then we clear the table of our agendas and work papers and go around the room to see how people are doing. In many companies, this is the chatter while people wait for everyone to get to the meeting. But here, it's the deliberate second half of our meeting. It's also when we have our core values and rules discussions. Let me walk you through an actual department meeting we held here several years ago, so you get the idea.

"We began the meeting at 11:00 in the morning. There were ten of us in the room, and this was a sales meeting for one of our regions. Bob Simpson, the regional manager, had eight of his salespeople in attendance who were his direct reports. Bob wanted me to show him how to conduct a 50/50 Meeting, as he had not done one before. I told him to hold his staff meeting for as long as it usually took. Using his **Business Goals** app with individual accomplishments and dates, he went around the room and asked people to report on where they were in reaching their goals. He asked them to report any problems with orders, customer service, shipping, reporting, and so forth. It was a pretty standard meeting, with some people achieving more than they had expected and others achieving less. His portion of the meeting was well run, to the point, and completed in approximately forty minutes. Then he handed it over to me and announced that I would be introducing a new portion to our meetings, 'The 50/50 Meeting' from the **Business Goals** class. I had a few pizzas brought in and asked people to clear away work papers. I casually asked how everyone was doing, and then, as if I was trying to break the ice, I simply asked what people had done last weekend. Little did they know it was a deliberate part of the meeting. I went around the room, starting with the person on my left, asking them to tell us as much or little as they cared about what they had done last Saturday and Sunday.

"We got halfway around the room with pretty normal stuff, like working in the yard, watching sports on TV, short outings with family members, or work around the house. Then we came to Francis. She said some family members had come into town, and she held an early Christmas that past weekend. It was clear she didn't want to elaborate, so we continued around the room. A few more regular weekends were shared, including one person who said he was out with his girlfriend looking at wedding rings. Everyone gave him some jabs about tying the knot. The whole process took about another forty minutes and was quite fun. That was it. We learned what each other did on the weekend. But two pieces of big news were uncovered. After the meeting was adjourned, I went to Francis. I asked her what was up with the early Christmas. She said her father was dying and he wouldn't make it to Christmas, his favorite holiday, so some of her family members flew into town to celebrate Christmas with him for the last time. I was able to tell her how sorry I was, which I wouldn't have had the chance to do without the 50/50 Meeting and following up."

A BAD SEASON

"So Todd, remember we talked about how sometimes people have bad seasons in their lives and how it affects their work performance? Well, I felt horrible. Francis was one of the few people in the meeting who did not make her sales goals. She had been a good employee who almost always did well. But recently, she had been noticeably late on several occasions, and she didn't appear to have her head in the game. Our standard method of operation would have been to tell her that we didn't know what was going on, but she needed to get to work on time and improve. Now I understood why her performance had dropped. I knew I had two choices: I could act like nothing was going on and press her to step up her performance, or I could try to help. Then a brilliant idea hit me that turned out to be one of the keys to our success. I went to Bob, her supervisor, and asked if he had any knowledge about Francis' early Christmas. He said no, so I filled him in. He, too, felt bad, especially since he had been putting pressure on her to perform and get to work on time. I asked him what would happen if we went to two of the other salespeople and asked them if they would help out, given the situation. I was sure they would. Then we could go to Francis and tell her that we wanted to give her Wednesday afternoons off so she could go and sit by her father's side until he passed away or improved.

"We approached two of Bob's other salespeople from his region and told them about the early Christmas. When they heard, before we could even ask, they asked if there was anything they could do. We said yes and suggested they cover for Francis on Wednesday afternoons. They thought it was a great idea.

"We then went to Francis and told her that Misty and Carl were going to cover for her on Wednesdays so she could leave at noon to be with her father. In tears, she said she appreciated the thought but didn't feel comfortable doing that. Death was scary to her, and she didn't know what it would be like to sit by his side every week for a few hours. We eventually convinced her to do it," Blake beamed.

"But Todd, we didn't realize what we had done. Our culture shifted with that one event. Bob became a support to Francis instead of an antagonist. Each week he asked her how things went with her father. Just asking the question was taking part of the burden off of Francis. Bob also wasn't so pushy when it came to her numbers. Once we found out about her situation, we knew her numbers would be off for some time. We could either support her through it or do what we had always done—tell her to 'get to work on time and keep your head in the game.' There was more that we didn't expect. She became very close friends with Carl and Misty, who were doing her job every Wednesday afternoon. Francis' father passed away within three months. A month later, Francis was coming out of her deep grief. But she was a different person. She told me that Severson Systems allowed her to spend some time with her father, which was perhaps the most important time in her life with him. Had he died without that time with her, she would have agonized over not spending his last days with him. In addition to that, she realized that Carl and Misty were the ones who allowed her to do this. They became very close friends and part of her support mechanism during the last days and through the funeral services. A friendship was formed that will never be broken. In addition, several other employees brought her meals on Wednesdays to take home, so she didn't have to cook for her family. The company rallied around Francis.

"What we didn't expect was who Francis became. Once she was back at work emotionally and physically, she was on fire for Severson. She almost doubled her best year's sales. She told every customer out there how great Severson was for helping her through that tough time. And she became an advocate for the firm with our employees. If anyone even started to say something negative about the company, she'd show them how and why they were wrong. We had developed a lifetime employee, and all we did was treat her like we would hope to be treated under the same circumstances. Francis went through a tough season in her life. We found there are bad and good seasons, both of which have the same potential impact on the company," Blake concluded.

"That is incredible. I've never heard of anything like it," Todd marveled.

A GOOD SEASON

"During that same meeting," continued Blake, "you'll remember that one of the guys was getting picked on because he was looking at wedding rings. Well, at the time, I didn't recognize it, but we were about to go through the exact same thing with him. His name was Tom. Tom was getting ready for his wedding, which was a few months away. And for about six weeks before his wedding, he became the same employee Francis was before we stepped in and helped her. Tom was regularly late for work, his sales numbers started to fall, and he just wasn't into his work. It was a tension-filled time for him and us. Then we realized he was going through a season just as Francis had, only it was a good season. As a result of Tom's situation, we now have a policy about weddings and seasons in general. Shortly after Tom's experience, we had another young lady, Connie, in accounting who was getting married. We went to the accounting department about two months before her wedding and asked if two or three people would not mind putting in a little extra effort on her behalf so we could give her Wednesday afternoons off to plan her wedding.

They agreed, and we gave her the time off. We allowed her to go and plan the most spectacular wedding ever.

"We could have been dense like we were with Tom and told her to get to work on time and get her head in the game. But instead, we told her to do the best she could when she was at work. And instead of taking time during work to make calls about the wedding, as Tom had done, she could now make those calls on Wednesday afternoons. It was a simple arrangement, but the outcome was far different from Tom's. At the wedding, she publicly thanked her supervisor, the co-workers who did her job on Wednesdays, and Severson Systems for being 'an awesome place to work.' When Connie got back from her honeymoon, she came into my office and personally thanked me for allowing her to plan and have the best wedding she could have imagined. Her performance in accounting did something similar to Francis's in sales. She was on fire for the company and told everyone what a great place it was to work and how some of her best friends in life worked there.

"Todd, we've realized that every person will go through a season or two. Some will be good, and some will be bad. Bad seasons are things like divorce, death, illness, and bankruptcy. Good seasons are getting married, having a baby, graduating from school, or moving into a new house. Good or bad, they both affect the person's job performance. Both can be very stressful. As a company, we have a choice. We can get angry and ignore the fact that people will undergo seasons, or we can support them. It doesn't cost us anything and has paid huge dividends over the years. The employee has been grateful to the company and their co-workers in nearly every case. We've developed a culture that is supportive of each other, and we've built lifetime employees who are dedicated and super-productive. It's been a major component in allowing people to enjoy those they work with.

"Oh, but there is one thing. Remember I said that nearly every employee is grateful to the company and the employees that help them through their season? Well, we've found that out of a hundred people, there might be one or two who take advantage of the system. They find out we help people going through seasons and somehow develop a season that lasts a lifetime. We've been able to ferret those out and move them on. In those cases, we've needed the help of our attorney, so we didn't end up in a lawsuit. But it's truly a small fragment of people who have this mindset. We decided it was worth it to continue the program instead of letting one or two percent of the people spoil it for the rest." Blake truly was proud of his employees. Todd could see it in the way Blake talked about them.

"Before you go, here are some keys to executing a successful Group 50/50 Meeting," said Blake, handing Todd a sheet of paper for him to study. "I look forward to hearing how your first group meeting goes."

HOW TO EXECUTE A SUCCESSFUL GROUP 50/50 MEETING

1. Allow people to respond to your questions only to the extent they feel comfortable.
2. Don't drill down if they don't want you to.
3. Don't ask personal questions.
4. Don't allow people to go too deeply in the group. Ask to take it offline if things get too detailed for the group setting.
5. Make sure you cover normal staff meeting items first, and the people side second.

CHAPTER SUMMARY

- There are two types of Group 50/50 Meetings:
  - The all-staff meeting
  - The department meeting
- The all-staff meeting should be a time of celebration for what's been accomplished and inform everyone about the great things happening at your organization.
- The department meeting should start with individual accomplishments and information about how the team can better reach their goals. The second half of the meeting should be spent seeing how the team is doing and allowing people to share what's going on in their lives that they want to share.
- The order of topics discussed at the Group 50/50 Meeting is essential:
  - The goals and accomplishments must be done first.
  - The people side must be done second.
- Become aware of what is appropriate and inappropriate to discuss in a 50/50 Meeting. Take sensitive items offline.
- Everyone will go through seasons in their lives. Some will be good, and some will be bad. We need to help people through the seasons in their lives and watch out for the advantage-takers.

POINTS TO PONDER

- Do you remember going through a season in your life (good or bad)?
  - How did it affect your productivity at work?
  - Did your employer support you through the season?
  - If not, how would you have liked to have been supported through that season? What would have helped you?
- If you know people around you are going through a difficult season of their lives, what ways can you help them?

18

DISCUSS THE RULES AND CORE VALUES

The following week, Blake covered an interesting component for group meetings, which had to do with rules and core values. "Todd, we use the Group 50/50 Meeting as a time to discuss the rules and core values we live by here at Severson. Remember I asked you for the rules you choose to live by, and you gave me a list? Then I gave you ten overarching principles we choose to live by here at Severson. We actually discuss both lists regularly so we can actively deploy our company policies and agree on what these rules and principles mean. I've found that if we don't do this, our morale dips. People like talking about the rules they wish to live by and how to get better at deploying them. It adds a layer of accountability that everyone wants," Blake told Todd.

"There are two ways we incorporate our rules and core values. The list you came up with is almost the same list that everyone else here came up with when they went through the same drill. You'll remember I've collected a list of characteristics and attributes from asking the question about the criteria you would use for choosing friends if you moved to a new city." Blake pulled a piece of paper out of his desk with about fifteen words on it and handed it to Todd. Todd recognized the attributes.

Important Characteristics and Attributes

honest	moral
loyal	caring/kind
considerate	fun
authentic	unselfish
reliable	visionary
responsible	intelligent
trustworthy	appreciative
forgiving	even-tempered
positive	

"This list helped us form the basic set of rules for how we want to treat each other. But we have to discuss them regularly because we might have different definitions or understandings of what each word means. The

50/50 Meeting helps us do this. For example, the first word on the list is 'honest.' Let me give you a picture of how two people could have different interpretations of honesty. When you were a kid, your mother may have told you, 'Don't play with Johnny; he's a bad apple.' Two weeks later, you call your mom on the phone and ask her if you can go to the mall with some friends. She asks who is going. You tell her, Billy, Cameron, Mike, and Stu. You don't tell her that Johnny is going, too. You reason that you told the truth because the other boys were, in fact, going. But you told the truth with the intent to deceive. Those boys were on your mother's approved list, so of course, she would allow you to go with them. Had you been fully honest and told her that Johnny was going too, she probably would not allow you to go. When you tell the truth to deceive, it's lying and is, therefore, not honest.

"So in our Group 50/50 Meetings, we talk about our rules to re-establish them and gain a common understanding for each one. There are no gray areas or excuses for not following them. Does that make sense?" Blake asked. Todd affirmed that he understood.

"Great," said Blake. "Sometimes, I'll do a write-up from a word on the list and have what I call a Value Discussion. These Value Discussions provide a common and consistent format for us to discuss issues. I just pick a topic and then provide talking points. Sometimes I'll list what we want to achieve and then show the opposite of each item. People here have become accustomed to hearing, 'We're going to have a Value Discussion,' and they know what that means. For the word 'authenticity,' I did a Value Discussion called, 'Are You Leading an Authentic Life?' We talked about it during that week's Group 50/50 Meetings. Here's a copy of what I handed out."

Authenticity: Are You Leading an Authentic Life?

Are you living an authentic life? If you're not, will you really be satisfied if you stop to examine your life? So many times, people try to be something they aren't, trying to impress others or to be in a place they don't belong. If you're not living an authentic life, you're a phony. Eventually, this will catch up to you, and you will experience guilt, depression, and anxiety. Start taking the steps today to be 100% you.

You are authentic if you...	You may not be authentic if you...
Tell it exactly like it is. Tell the Truth.	Embellish, exaggerate, or flat-out lie.
Allow no one to feel inferior due to your perceived wealth, intellect, or accomplishments.	Flaunt what you believe to be wealth, intellect, or accomplishments.
Accept the positives in everyone you meet and consider them no better of worse than yourself.	Think you are better than others for any reason (i.e., personal wealth, intellect, or education).
Do what you say you will do when you say you will do it.	Don't follow through.
Allow people to accept you for who you are.	Hope to impress people with what you have or what you have done.
Live within your means debt free.	Overspend or have what you have only because you've borrowed to get it.
Do things for self-improvement.	Do things to impress others.
Do things out of respect for what's right.	Do things based on what feels good.
Know exactly where you stand on issues.	Let society influence you.

Before anyone will take us seriously or want to become our friend, we must be honest with ourselves and acquire the qualities listed in the first column. Eliminate anything in the second column that you are now doing. Then see how you have changed your own perspective as well as how others perceive you. Do this consciously for the next week!

"We also do Value Discussions using the **Business Goals** core values posted around the office. They tell us how we should behave and set the boundaries for that behavior. You've seen these before," said Blake, pointing to the framed list on his wall.

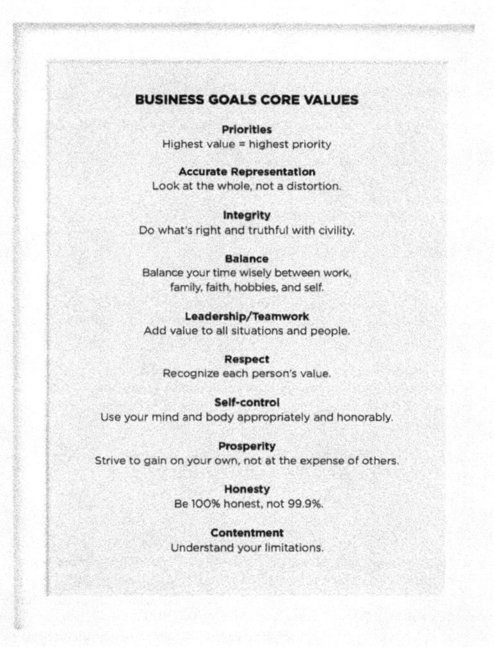

BUSINESS GOALS CORE VALUES

Priorities
Highest value = highest priority

Accurate Representation
Look at the whole, not a distortion.

Integrity
Do what's right and truthful with civility.

Balance
Balance your time wisely between work, family, faith, hobbies, and self.

Leadership/Teamwork
Add value to all situations and people.

Respect
Recognize each person's value.

Self-control
Use your mind and body appropriately and honorably.

Prosperity
Strive to gain on your own, not at the expense of others.

Honesty
Be 100% honest, not 99.9%.

Contentment
Understand your limitations.

Next, Blake handed Todd a paper with "Core Value One: Priorities" written at the top. Todd was eager to hear more about how this all tied together. Blake explained, "Not long ago, I did a Value Discussion on 'priorities,' the first core value from the **Business Goals** program. You can talk about many topics surrounding priorities, but I chose to do this one on time management. It was very eye-opening. Even though this study was done years ago, I believe the numbers haven't changed much. Every year or two, I do the same search, and I still find the same time-wasters on everyone's list in about the same percentages. I just like how thorough this study is and how it correlates wasting time to cost. I know the cost is much higher today, but the distraction areas remain the same."

Core Value One: Priorities

Time Management

Do we really expect you to work an eight-hour workday?

In 2005, Salary.com surveyed corporate Human Resource managers and found that companies assume that their employees waste 0.94 hours per day. But when the employees were surveyed, they admitted to actually wasting 2.09 hours per day. For the average worker, that adds up to $6,720 each year in wasted salary dollars. For an American workforce of 132 million people, that's $759 billion dollars a year.

So what did people claim as their top time-wasting activities?

- Surfing the internet (personal use) = 44.7% (of the 10,044 people surveyed)
- Socializing with co-workers = 23.4%
- Conducting personal business = 6.8%
- Spacing out = 3.9%
- Running errands = 3.1%
- Making personal phone calls = 2.3%
- Applying for other jobs = 1.3%
- Planning personal events = 1.0%
- Arriving late or leaving early = 1.0%[1]

Living up to our core values means putting the right people and activities in the right order. We get to decide how we spend our time and there are all kinds of pressures and temptations to focus on the wrong things.

- There will be pressure to focus on personal things at work.
- There will be pressure to focus on work issues during family time.
- There will be pressure to pay attention to worthless things and ignore important relationships.

But living up to this core value of Priorities means using "on-the-clock" time for work and saving your personal business for scheduled breaks or after the workday ends.

Tough Questions

- Do you ever use "on-the-clock time" to do any of the activities listed above? If you do, why?
- Who benefits from your unethical use of "on-the-clock" time? Who loses out? How?
- Do you struggle to balance your personal and professional responsibilities?
- Are there reasonable ways in which our organization could be more supportive and flexible in alleviating that pressure?
- In what ways does wasting "on-the-clock" time also violate our organizational policies or the law?

"We learned something else when we deployed this Value Discussion on time management. When people violate core values or rules, it brings down the performance of the entire organization. When people see someone else taking care of personal business on company time or surfing the internet for personal stuff, other employees feel entitled to do the same thing or feel they aren't going to work as hard if people around them are not going to work hard by stealing company time. The same was true of every core value. When they get violated by one person, they are more apt to get violated by many people. We found the opposite to be true too. When everyone is doing their best to live up to our core values, we hold each other accountable and call each other out when we see violations, and the morale and work ethic rises," Blake explained.

"Wow," Todd remarked. "I can see why these Value Discussions would be useful. Pretty much just lays everything out there, black and white."

"That's right," said Blake, "you're getting the idea. We must build into our Group 50/50 Meeting a discussion about core values because it also helps us maintain our focus on the third most important thing employees want in the workplace. When we discuss core values regularly, it becomes easier to live up to them. But there is another benefit. When our customers see the framed core values, they start asking questions. It gives our people a chance to explain them, sort of a teaching opportunity, and it's become something that sets us apart from our competition. It has the same impact when we interview people for jobs. Potential employees see the framed core values and comment on them. We've become the place people want to work because rules and core values are important to us."

"Well, as a matter of fact," said Todd, "I thought it was impressive when I saw those core values as I toured your facilities for the first time. It had an impact on me too." He felt very lucky to be a part of this company.

"I'm glad. I always like to hear that it continues to work," said Blake. "Now, let me get back to some final points on our rules and core values. We didn't want to be a little more honest than our competition; we wanted an absolute bar. Everyone here wants us to hold them accountable and vice versa. Inviting our employees, vendors, and customers to hold us accountable to our rules and core values builds trust. It sets us apart from our competition as an employer, as a customer to our vendors, and our customers. I really want you to take our rules and core values here seriously."

Their meeting was over, and Blake walked Todd to the door. Shaking hands, Blake said, "When you go home tonight, tell your family about our rules and core values, then when you come back next week, I'll teach you about the One-on-One 50/50 Meeting."

Todd went home that night and told his family about the Group 50/50 Meeting and the company's rules and core values. Friday night was becoming a family night at the Hanson home. Sure, Scott and Anne went out after dinner, but they came to enjoy the time spent with their parents. More importantly, they liked the changes they saw in their dad.

CHAPTER SUMMARY

- We all want rules and core values in life. It is the number three thing employees want in the workplace.
- There are ten basic core values we all want and expect from others:
    - — priorities
    - — accurate representation
    - — integrity
    - — balance
    - — leadership/teamwork
    - — respect
    - — self-control
    - — prosperity
    - — honesty
    - — contentment
- When our actions align with our core values, we feel successful, confident, and fulfilled.

- The Group 50/50 Meeting is the perfect way to discuss rules and core values using Value Discussions.
- We needed to be constantly reminded of the rules and core values so everyone is on the same page and there are no gray areas about what they mean.

POINTS TO PONDER

- What rules do you want to follow or need to be followed in the workplace? At home?
- Does your place of work have a clear, published set of rules or core values for its employees to live by? What about your home?
- What ideas do you have for Value Discussions in your home or workplace? How can you present this idea to leadership? How will you incorporate them into your leadership if you are the leader?

19

THE ONE-ON-ONE 50/50 MEETING

THE LEFT SIDE OF THE EQUATION

The following week, Todd reported to Blake's office as usual. He gave a brief download on how well his family had received the Group 50/50 Meeting and the rules and core values. Todd ran his family through the scenario for determining the rules people want in life. He was blown away when his family said they wanted to follow those rules too. He had completed his first Group 50/50 Meeting earlier in the week and said it had gone very well. Blake was pleased with the progress Todd was making. His life was changing just as it had with the other employees. Now it was time to learn about the One-on-One 50/50 Meeting.

"Todd, I can't emphasize enough that the 50/50 Meetings are our key to success. They are the key tools in helping employees fulfill the contract and enjoy the people they work with. We work hard to develop relationships with them, which means we must spend a focused amount of attention on the people around us. We pursue them to determine their needs and then do our best to meet those needs. Does that make sense?" Blake asked.

"It does," Todd responded.

"Okay, good. Now let me explain the One-on-One 50/50 Meeting," said Blake. "As with the Group 50/50 Meeting, there are two components to the one-on-one meeting, with an equal amount of time allocated to each component:

1. Show the employee what they need to do to succeed in their position (left side of the equation).
2. Invest yourself in the lives of each person on your team (right side of the equation).

"Like with the Group 50/50 Meeting, there are some important guidelines to running the One-on-One 50/50 Meeting well. First off, your meeting will only be with the people that report directly to you. If any of your direct reports have people that report to them, they should be holding their own one-on-ones. Because of the need to meet with each person who directly reports to you weekly, the absolute maximum number of people who directly report to you should be no greater than thirty. Ideally, the number of direct reports to any one person should be twelve or less. It would help if you held your one-on-ones weekly. Bi-weekly is okay, but not as good. These meetings can be fairly prompt, lasting only five or ten minutes or as long as an hour. We've found that the ideal meeting is between twenty and thirty minutes.

"Before the meeting starts, it's essential that you remember your role. In this case, you are the coach of your employees. Imagine being the head coach of a professional basketball team. You coach some of the best players in the world. Your job is to take great players and make them better. Help them improve the things they are good at and help them work through the things they aren't so good at. You must put yourself in the mindset of a coach, not a dictator. You can't dictate that your NBA All-Star goes out and scores forty points. But you can coach him into scoring more and more points per game. So your first task is to look back over your list of the attributes of a great mentor and do your best to be those things for your employee during the meeting—encouraging, teaching, good listener, available, disciplinarian when necessary, rewarding when appropriate, etc.," said Blake as he handed Todd another copy of the mentor/coach attributes.

The Perfect Mentor/Coach

Honest	Personable	Focused
Moral	Rewarding	Humble
Authentic	Disciplining	Forgiving
High level of integrity	Encouraging	Recognizes my skills
Respected	Experienced	Empathetic
Visionary	Communicative	Supportive
Positive	Courageous	Strategic
Friendly	Driven	Reasonable
Empowering	Patient	Brings out the best in me
Sensible	Intelligent	
Comforting	Fair	
Teaching	Caring	

WHEN AND WHERE TO HOLD THE MEETING

"Schedule your One-on-One Meeting when you both can take the time, and it will be uninterrupted. Pick the slowest part of the week, not twenty minutes during crunch time. Your meeting place should be where you won't be interrupted. Many people meet outside the office for coffee. Others hold them in their offices or their normal work area, but make sure you can give the person your full attention. Even a video conference call works. It's important to see the other person to read how you both are responding to the other. The location isn't important if you aren't interrupted or distracted by your phone, email, or other people. Oh, one last thing. If your direct report is a woman, make sure you hold your One-on-One in a place that isn't intimate. Don't go to a bar after work or behind closed doors in your office. We don't want people to become unfaithful to their marriages because of these meetings, and we don't want to give people wrong impressions. Be very cautious about this, Todd," urged Blake.

SUCCESS IN YOUR POSITION THROUGH SETTING EXPECTATIONS

"So, let's start with the left side of the equation part of the meeting.

Do you remember how in Step One of the **Business Goals** program that everyone sets personal goals that support our corporate annual goals? We use the **Business Goals** app to allow our employees to develop their lists of priorities and weights and tie them to our corporate goals. You always have instant access to their lists through the app and can see what they are working on, their progress, and which goal they have tied it to. If you see something way out of bounds in terms of either priority order or weight, you can change it in the app or connect with them to discuss it. If you make a change, they will receive a notification indicating you've made a change to their priority list. Though you can make changes through the app without speaking to them, I've found it's best when you can recommend changes during your one-on-one meeting," Blake told Todd.

"We set the accomplishment or due date for goals based on the individual. Some employees have to set goals that are due twice a day, once in the morning and once after lunch. We typically do this with a new employee working in a production environment where success in the job is based on the quantity and quality of work being done. They go over with teammates what they have to accomplish by noon, and if they accomplish it, they can come back after lunch. After lunch, they have a new set of objectives to accomplish by the end of the day. If they meet the task, we invite them back the next day. On the other extreme, we have had outside salespeople set monthly goals. It all depends on how capable they are of setting goals and objectives and carrying them out," Blake explained.

"During the first several weeks of your one-on-ones, I recommend that you have your direct reports set new goals in their apps by Friday for the following week. Have them walk you through the process they used to determine which tasks they want to accomplish by the next meeting—their top four or five in priority order and weighted. Then have them develop a specific accomplishment for each priority. Hopefully, they come up with a list that makes good sense to you. If not, you'll need to help them understand which things need to be done this week so you can accomplish your goals. Like a good coach, you should be encouraging them for the way they thought it through unless they just missed it. If that's the case, I will naturally challenge you on why they are on the team. Everyone on your team has been here for a while and is used to the process I've just explained. It should go pretty smoothly," said Blake.

"You can look at this as a negotiation. The most important thing is that you agree on the top four or five things you would like them to accomplish, in what order, and weight. Equally important is what they won't be doing. If you agree on which things need to be completed, you are telling them that the remainder of the items on their lists beyond the top four or five don't have to be completed in the next week. If you are crystal clear on exactly what the accomplishment looks like by what time and date, then there's a better chance they will complete it. One of the biggest mistakes is when managers try to have their team accomplish more than four or five things at a time. That is a recipe for failure. The more things a person has on their list, the fewer they are likely to complete. They will also work through the list in the order they want and what is the most fun for them instead of the most important. This is often not the same order the manager expects. The employee gets stressed with too much to do yet cannot accomplish anything. One of the definitions for stress I've always liked is 'when desire outpaces resources.' If you give someone a long list of things to accomplish, they will desire to accomplish everything on the list to please you. When their resource of time isn't enough to complete the tasks, they end up stressed," Blake explained.

STRESS OCCURS WHEN DESIRE OUTPACES RESOURCES.

Continuing, Blake said, "There is one compromise position to consider. You may determine the top three or four things to be completed during the timeframe, but you also agree that they should touch certain things on their lists beyond the top three or four, but they don't necessarily need to get them completed. To show you this visually, let's look at the app." Blake brought up the app on his phone, went to his direct reports, and brought up what Gwen Thomas was working on that week.

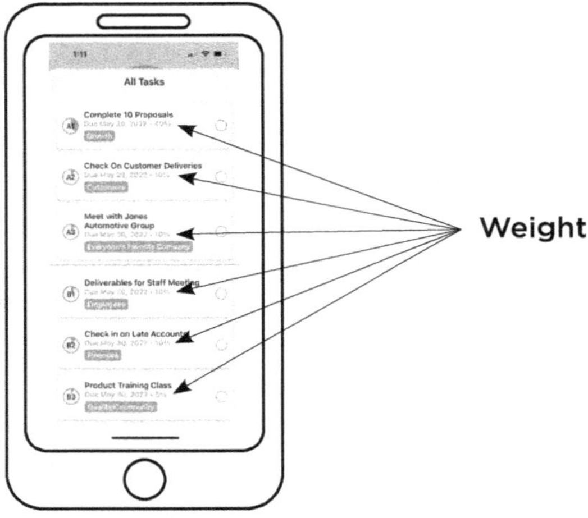

"This is from one of our salespeople, Gwen. You can see that the most important thing on her list was to complete the ten proposals due that week. It was rated number one with a 40% weight, so she should spend as much as 40% of her time on it. You can see items two through five and the weight of each one. You will note that the top five only add up to 85%. That's because we wanted her to spend 15% of her time doing something for items six to nine so they don't become big problems by putting them off for a week or more. In many cases, it's simply a phone call or email for each item to keep them active. Other times it's following up on something that's in progress but can't be completed yet because you are waiting for someone else to deliver something," Blake explained. "It's very important that you set realistic expectations. Be sure that the average person in the same position can accomplish the expectations you set with the same competency. Your goal is to agree upon what can be accomplished by what date and in what order. Be as specific as possible."

THE GRADING SYSTEM

"So how do you know what success looks like? You need to tell your team in very empirical terms. Think about it this way. When you were in school, most teachers told you what it took to get an A, B, C, D, or F. An A was 90%, B was 80%, etc. We were taught this system for at least twelve years of our life and then stopped when we graduated from school. But we brought that system back into our workplace because we want our employees to know how they are doing every week. We attached a scoring system to their weekly goals. Why? Because in those same studies on employee satisfaction, they found that employees wanted feedback on how they were doing on a regular basis. That's not an annual review. Some companies do their annual reviews every two or three years. Here employees know where they stand weekly. Then their quarterly scores are no surprise when it comes to their goals and expectations."

"So people here know how they are doing on a weekly basis?" Todd asked.

"You bet they do. I'll walk you through our scoring system in our last meeting. But for today, all you need to know is this: people here can't underperform for three weeks in a row without a corrective action plan. In fact, as you will see, supervisors seldom fire employees; the employees fire themselves. More on that in a few minutes," Blake responded.

Todd looked surprised and was intrigued by this concept.

"Let's go back to Gwen's expectations," said Blake. "It's easy to assign a scoring system to her top five goals. For her first expectation, she had to complete ten proposals that week. We could have assigned this scoring system to her number one item:

SCORING SYSTEM	A = 10 Proposals (100%) B = 8 Proposals (80%) C = 7 Proposals (70%) D = 6 Proposals (60%) F = 5 Proposals (50%)

"With this system, it is very easy for Gwen to know where she stands. She would get strong praises if she were to come back in a week with ten or more proposals completed. She also knows in advance how we will react if she only came in with six proposals completed," Blake explained.

"What really makes this system work is that we let the employee set the expectation, the scoring system, and the consequences, and we simply provide coaching or feedback. You already know that we ask the employees to come up with their own goals and expectations. Our hope is that because of their competency levels, they can develop expectations on their own that are at least 80% of what we would come up with had we dictated our expectations to them. Let me explain why this is important.

"If you grew up in California, you know that in the fourth grade, you studied California missions. Often students are required to build a model of a mission as part of their curriculum. There are two ways that can happen. They can go home and tell their parents that they have to build a mission, and the parent can say, 'I know exactly how we're going to do that. We're going to take sugar cubes and Elmer's glue and build this thing up.' Then the parent actually builds it. It looks great, but the student is dejected because they didn't build it. The parent dictated how it would be built. Conversely, the parent can encourage the student to build the mission however they want and, along the way, provide cursory advice on how it could look better. The student is much happier because they built it and only got coaching from someone with more experience.

"The same thing is true for employees. They want to create something for the company using the time, talent, and expertise for which they were hired. So we let them create their own goals and coach them along the way to match our corporate goals. Then we ask them to tell us how it should be scored. Each week when the employee uses the app and develops their expectations for the week, we also have them set the scoring system. If the scoring seems a little low, we simply tell them we think they can do better and encourage them to raise their numbers to where we want them. But we allow them to negotiate and tell us why they think it needs to be where they suggested. The bottom line is this—if they design it, there's a better chance they will achieve it. It follows what you heard so many times in the Business Goals class, 'People will support what they help develop.' And the proof is in our numbers," Blake said confidently.

PEOPLE WILL SUPPORT WHAT THEY HELP DEVELOP.

"We allow our employees to weigh in on what levels they must hit for bonuses, raises, and promotions. When you ask an employee what score they should be hitting to simply fulfill their contract, keep their job, and get paid, the number is usually pretty high, like 80% or better. They need to be doing good work, which most would agree is 80%. The process is great because we never get employees asking for raises who aren't performing at very high levels. Employees know where they stand at all times because everyone can see it on the app. It also makes it very easy to give bonuses and promotions because we always can see where people are performing."

ACCEPTING THE CONSEQUENCES

Blake went on. "Not only do we want the employee to set the expectation and assess their scoring weekly, but we also want them to set the consequence—even as far as firing themselves. We are very encouraging when an employee develops a good set of expectations and then reaches 80% or better for what they hoped to accomplish. We also follow a specific process when they don't meet their goals.

"If Jack Welch from GE had used this system, he would have never had to put his managers through the task of picking the employees in the bottom 10%. The employees would have known themselves, as would their managers and supervisors, because they could all see it on the app. Many of our public and private schools provide real-time assessments of their students. We're bringing that same methodology into the workplace," said Blake.

"Now, let's talk about what happens when an employee doesn't hit their numbers. When an employee performs at less than 80%, we start a three-step corrective action plan. First, everyone here knows that we want scores that are 75% or better. Less than this, and they know they are C-level employees, and they will be the first to go. When a score hits 75%, we simply ask them what they think the consequence should be if they hit that same number next week or the next time they agree to meet. Usually, the employee will prescribe disciplinary measures that are worse than you may come up with on your own. If they miss it a second time, we ask them what should happen if they miss it three times in a row. Let me give you a real-life example. We had a facilities manager here who wasn't hitting his expectations. His manager sat down with him, and they both came up with the minimum expectations to fulfill the duties of the job. The goals were clearly laid out using Step One of the **Business Goals** program, and the top three or four priorities were agreed upon by priority and weight. The facilities manager agreed that he could do everything on the list. These were pretty simple things; either he did them or didn't. He stated that if he couldn't do them after three chances, he would leave his keys on the table and resign. For the first two weeks, he provided some excuses for why he couldn't accomplish the tasks at hand. When we asked what should happen if he missed it the third week in a row, he again said he'd leave. He resigned after the third week. We were not the bad guys. He admitted he was incapable of meeting the minimum requirements for the job. With this system, an employer shouldn't have to fire employees. They will fire themselves," Blake said with a smile.

"There was one other caveat to this situation. We made sure there wasn't something going on in the facility manager's personal life preventing him from accomplishing his job. The first week he didn't hit his numbers, and his manager asked if anything was going on, either at work or outside of work, that was interfering with him being able to complete the tasks they had agreed upon. There wasn't," said Blake. "If there were, we would have followed our protocol for dealing with good or bad seasons—we would have come alongside him somehow."

POSITIVE CONSEQUENCES

"We really believe it's more important that we provide the right response when the employee hits their goal than the corrective action when they don't. You already know that people respond better to positive responses than negative ones. So when an employee reaches 80% of their expectations, we praise them. Remember, the role of the supervisor is that of a mentor. When you look at the attributes of a mentor, they are synonymous with the roles of a parent. Employees want to please their supervisors in the same way children want to please their parents. They want to meet their parents' expectations, and when they do, they want affectionate praise. We're not going to give hugs and kisses to our employees for doing a good job, but we will shake their hands and tell them they are valuable members of our team and are doing a great job. This component is a key ingredient to employees enjoying the people they work with, much like how children will enjoy being with their parents if they please them on a regular basis and vice versa. If the parent only dictates and disciplines, the child will not want to please the parent and just want the provision. 'Just give me food, clothes, roof, and transportation I need to survive, and the moment I'm able, I'm out of here,' is the attitude of a child whose parents don't understand what they really want. Children want parents who pursue them, seek to please them, and meet their needs. I can't emphasize this enough. We want to be an encouraging place to work, so we strive to reward good work. We don't take good work for granted. Make sure you get this," Blake said firmly.

CHAPTER SUMMARY

- The maximum number of people who report to you should be less than thirty...the ideal is 10–12.
- One-on-One 50/50 Meetings should take place once a week.
  — Every other week will work; weekly is best.
- The meeting should occur during the slowest part of your day and week.

- You can hold a 50/50 Meeting anywhere, as long as it allows focused attention on each other.
- It's best if you can see each other during the meeting. In-person is best, video conference is okay, and phone calls should be avoided unless it's the only way to connect.
- The ideal meeting is twenty to thirty minutes, but even a five-minute meeting is okay if that's all you have time for that day.
- Your 50/50 Meetings will only be with the people that directly report to you.
- Remember your role as a coach before you start your meeting. Review the attributes.
- The first half of a One-on-One 50/50 Meeting is to set and align expectations, the left side of the equation.
- There is a grading system for performance.
- There are consequences for performance—good and bad.

POINTS TO PONDER

- How many people report to your boss in addition to you?
- How many people report to you?
- Are you holding one-on-one meetings on a regular basis (weekly)?
- Are you clear about what you need to accomplish and what you won't be accomplishing?
- How about for those who report to you?
- When people do a good job, do you encourage them with accolades?
- When people don't perform according to expectations, what are the consequences? Who sets them?

20

THE ONE-ON-ONE 50/50 MEETING

THE RIGHT SIDE OF THE EQUATION

"Okay, Todd, now that we've thoroughly discussed the left side of the equation for the One-on-Ones, now we'll talk about the right side—the people part. It's essential that you conduct your one-on-ones in this order. You agree on what they need to do to be successful in their position—the left side—then you talk about life—whatever the person you're meeting with wants to talk about. You want the person to leave saying, 'He showed me exactly what I needed to do to be successful in my position, and then he genuinely was interested in me as a person.' In the Group 50/50 Meeting, the goal is for people to get to know each other on more than an acquaintance level and continually discuss the rules. In the one-on-one meeting, the goal is to talk about how life is going, personal interests, and determine if anything is happening in the person's life that would prevent them from being successful and how we might help them through," Blake explained.

"Remember, the right side of the equation is simply doing life with people in a way that builds the relationship. It's about caring for and treating people how we want to be cared for and treated, caring more for the people around us than being selfish and thinking about ourselves. We want to do life with them in a way that we couldn't imagine doing life without them. It's about creating lifelong friendships and a community based on what's good and right—helping each other live up to the rules and core values from the **Business Goals** program and the list we've created here at Severson. But all of this won't happen on its own. It happens because we are deliberate about recognizing what's important and then working on those things every day. We prioritize and weigh the most important things to us and everyone around us. It's about getting involved in the lives of everyone around us at a deeper level. Not just talking about the weather, sports, or the junk we hear in the news, but focusing on more important things in life, like our families, friendships, personal interests, and doing the things necessary to protect and further those relationships in a positive way. Sorry, I get very passionate about this topic because I know how important it is," said Blake. Todd smiled, knowing Blake truly believed what he preached. He hoped he would develop that kind of passion for all this.

"So here's how you do it," Blake continued. "Once you've aligned expectations, you need to put away your work papers and just talk about life. You can simply start with the question, 'What are you most excited about in life right now?' We will not pry into a person's private life any more than they want to share. However, I can tell you that if you show an interest, nearly everyone wants to share what they are excited about. It's human nature. People want to share their pains and gains with the people around them, especially their friends. So, you might start by asking, 'What was the best thing that happened this past week?' followed by, 'What was the worst thing that happened this past week?' People want a venue to share what they're excited about and sometimes what they are unhappy about. We don't pry; we only ask vague questions. They can respond however they want. My experience is that most of the time, better than 90% of people will be in a pretty good and positive season. Your weekly discussions will be about their families and what their kids or other family members are doing or interested in. You'll be discussing their hobbies and how they enjoy spending their time when they aren't at work. I find it very interesting to hear what people are interested in and the other things they've become experts in outside of work. You'll find the people around you are interesting and that you can learn many things from them just as they will be learning from you. Your life will become richer by knowing everyone you have a

50/50 conversation with," said Blake.

EARN TRUST, DON'T VIOLATE IT

"Todd, people will share so many different aspects of their lives with you, not because you've pried but because they want to share those things and have a deeper relationship with you. But we must protect what we are hearing and what people are sharing with us. People will trust you with many parts of their lives that they want to share with you, but you must earn that trust. They will want to share things they are very excited about and may want to unload their biggest problems. As the mentor, coach, or parent, you need to understand how to deal with some of the information. People will trust you with confidences that are sometimes sensitive in nature. The world doesn't need to know about some of the things you hear. When employees tell you something, you need to ask them what can be shared with their team and which things they prefer didn't leave the room. This is extremely important. This often goes sideways in companies when an employee shares something in confidence with another employee who then tells someone else. Pretty soon, a gossip chain starts, and there are unhappy and hurt people. We don't allow that here. You need to be crystal clear with your employees. If someone tells you something, you must get their permission to tell others if it's necessary to include the others in helping the person through a season. That is, of course, unless it's illegal, and then it must be reported to the proper authorities. If you hear anything related to child abuse or physical abuse of another person or animal, you must inform the person that this must be reported to the police. Then pick up the phone and call the police. Hopefully, this won't happen very often, and you will only get the other kinds of problems people typically have.

"Let me give you a real-life example. We had an employee, Janice, who came to me and told me her husband had a drug and gambling problem. She was a good employee, but we saw the signs in her performance. She finally told us during a one-on-one what was going on and that she didn't want her fellow employees to know. We agreed that we would tell the employees that Janice was simply going through a difficult season in her life and needed our support. We treated it exactly the same as the dying parent and the wedding seasons we've already talked about. We gave Janice time off for counseling appointments and other times when she had to deal with the situation. After a few months, Janice told us she was getting a divorce. We told her team that her situation was going from bad to worse, and she would need even more support. The team didn't know the details but respected her desire to keep the problem to herself. Eventually, she was able to tell her co-workers who were filling in for her while she was dealing with attorneys and a broken heart. We supported her through the process, and a few years later, Janice remarried. Who do you think was at her wedding?" Blake asked.

Todd shook his head and shrugged.

"Her two teammates who were doing her job while she was going through the divorce," Blake replied.

"The point is that we need to hold certain things in confidence and agree on what we will say to other people if we need their help. Because we've been doing this program here for some time, everyone understands the One-on-One 50/50 Meeting. In the very beginning, we had to earn trust and get permission to share. We know that sometimes people will need to keep things confidential, and other times they will be looking for their co-workers to help them through a season. This has to be done on a one-on-one basis. We didn't announce that the company was introducing a new program to help everyone through their personal problems. If we did that, we would have employees giving reasons why they couldn't perform that week. They'd look for the company and their co-workers to help them through everyday struggles. Instead, we simply started the program and individually asked people in their One-on-Ones what they were most excited about, what they were least excited about, and how things were going in their lives.

"It's very important that you don't pry into someone's personal life or state your opinion about what they tell you. If someone wants to talk about a subject of a personal nature, such as sex, God, family situations, and so forth, it is important you understand the laws we are guided by and our company policies. We are an equal opportunity employer, and we will not discriminate against anyone for their religious preferences, sexual preferences, age, gender, political affiliation, or other characteristics. If employees are in a season of life and we can help them through it as fellow human beings, we want to do that. But we need to use good judgment in the process. We won't allow people to take advantage of us, and we won't tolerate people making their problems our problems. You will find it's a fine line we walk. In general, there are a few tests you can run to see if getting involved makes sense or if the person is trying to use us."

THE EIGHT TESTS FOR GOOD DECISION MAKING

"In the **Business Goals** class, their 'Eight Tests for Good Decision Making' has become widely used here at Severson and is very valuable. Whenever I face a tough decision, I refer to the Eight Tests. I've found it helps when people come to me with their problems, and I can point them to the tests. Do we as a company need to help the person through a season?" Blake pulled out a card from his wallet that he had received in the **Business Goals** class and handed it to Todd. It had the "Eight Tests" on it:

Eight Tests for Good Decision Making

1. Do you have a sense of peace (no yuck feeling) as you ponder the problem?
2. If you were to consult books that gave great advice on the issue, what would the advice be?
3. If you talked to two or three people in positions of authority on the topic, what would they advise?
4. If you talked to two or three people who were very wise, what would they advise?
5. Is there a logical opportunity for resolution?
6. Are the provisions available for the resolution?
7. Does it make sense?
8. If you are married, what does your spouse say?

"At Severson, we use the **CAP** tests we talked about earlier (conscience, announcement, profit) on the cursory level and these eight tests as a more thorough way of making decisions. Both have served us well and have kept us from making some major mistakes. So, in the case of Francis, the one whose father was dying, if we heard her situation for the first time and ran them through the tests, the method we chose to resolve it made more sense than telling her to get to work on time and keep her head in the game. If we ran our decision to give her Wednesdays off through these tests, it would have been crystal clear that we were making the best decision. Let's compare that to someone we believe wants to take advantage of our goodwill. Say a team member came into your office and told you she was going through a tough time. She can't pay her bills, can't keep her car running properly, and isn't eating very well. All of this leads to continual tardiness and absences. Yet you've observed her spending money foolishly on clothes and drinks after work. What do you think the eight tests would tell us?"

"The first test alone would give the answer," Todd reasoned.

"Exactly. She's not in a bad season; she's giving excuses!" said Blake. "When running the eight tests, remember to look for one of the three answers we were taught in the **Business Goals** program. The three possible answers are a green light because you have a positive response to all eight tests. The second is a red light because you fail on one or more of the tests, so you don't move forward. The third is a yellow light. The yellow light is when you get several positive responses to the tests, like six or seven out of the eight, but you don't have a green light on the final one or two tests, and it's not because it's a failure on those one or two.

"Let me give you an example. You get positive responses to everything about a situation except the provision part. There isn't a provision you see to make it happen, but you feel positive about the other seven tests. This would be a yellow light, which means 'pause.' We don't dismiss the idea; we just don't put it into action until we get the final test—the provision. In real life, this might manifest itself when you are looking to buy a house or a car. You may have the vision and thought that you are supposed to buy a house or a car. You work through all eight tests, and the idea passes every test, except you don't have enough money for the down payment...which would be the provision. It doesn't mean you are supposed to discard the vision and not buy the house or car; it just means you need to wait until you save enough for the down payment, so the provision is met. Too often, we get visions or ideas, run the tests, and then force the issue when we don't pass all eight, and then everything goes wrong. Wait until you get all eight before you move forward. These eight tests have helped my life become more black and white and eliminated the gray. When whatever I'm thinking about doing passes all eight tests, I do it...it always works out. I can't emphasize enough how these eight tests will help you both at work and home," Blake told Todd.

CHAPTER SUMMARY

- The order of the One-on-One is vital: the left side first, then the right side.
- The goal of the second half of the meeting is to walk through life with people and, to a lesser degree, determine if there's something that would prevent someone from accomplishing their goals.
- If there is something, determine if we need to support the person through the issues.
- We want to treat and support others how we want to be treated and supported.
- People will open up only if they know it's a safe environment and their confidence in you won't be violated.
- There are eight tests we can use for making good decisions. You must have eight out of eight if you want a good outcome; less than eight means either don't do it or wait until you have all eight.

POINTS TO PONDER

- When you have learned people were going through tough seasons, how have you helped and encouraged them through that season?
- Are you good at holding confidential information to yourself?
  - If not, how will you ever earn trust from people?
- Will you use the eight tests to help you make good decisions?
  - Don't settle for four or five out of the eight. Wait until you have all eight to move forward.

BONUS

QR CODES AND LINK TO WATCH 8 TESTS VIDEO AND DOWNLOAD 8 TESTS CARD.

8 Tests Video

8 Tests Card

21

ATTITUDE IS EVERYTHING

Blake was nearing the end of Step Three, but there was one more strategy he needed to explain before he let Todd go for the day. "Todd, there's another component I want to add that I think will help you going forward. Do you remember the 85/15 Test we use to evaluate people's strengths? There's a similar test I use that relates to the overall attitude of people. Because of our own attitudes, we will impact the people around us and, in many cases, be able to shape their attitudes. There are two attitudes we can convey—positive or negative. Unfortunately, most people are not deliberate about which attitude they are conveying, which leads them to the default attitude, which I believe is a slightly negative attitude. Yet attitude is critical in the direction of a person and a company. Having the right attitude is key to approaching both the right and left sides of the equation we've been discussing. We will accomplish so much more in life, fulfilling the contract and enjoying the relationships, if we can be deliberate about living on the 85% side that is positive. Let me prove this to you by asking you a few questions. First, let's look at fulfilling the contract. If you look at the top four or five things you are supposed to accomplish this week and think that you'll never be able to do them, do you think that might impact your ability to do them?" Blake asked.

“Of course,” Todd responded.

“If you go into a 50/50 Meeting or you go home with a bad attitude because your day hasn’t gone the way you wanted, or you are letting something you’ve heard bother you, do you think it will have an impact on the person you’re having the 50/50 with or your family when you get home?”

“Definitely,” Todd responded.

“If you think about it for a few minutes, would you rather be around positive people or negative people?” Blake asked. “I know it’s almost a silly question. When people think about it, everyone would rather be around someone positive instead of someone negative. So let me explain why people tend to be negative, including you, and what you can do to change it. First, you can instantly tell whether a person lives in the positive 85% or the negative 15% simply by asking them how they are doing or what they generally talk about throughout the day. My experience is that people are generally negative and live in the 15% because we’ve been indoctrinated to live there. We live in a time where we only hear about the 15%. The news, internet, social media, podcasts, blogs, television, and radio generally focus on the 15% that’s gone wrong, is not working right, who’s been taken advantage of, and who’s to blame. We are indoctrinated by the bad news to the extent that we start living in the negative 15%. We complain about the negative 15% more than we recognize the positive 85%. It can become our personality. If we only listen to bad news, and that’s primarily what we talk about, it’s difficult not to become depressed, unproductive, cynical, and not enjoyable to be around. Our general response to anything becomes about why it won’t work or who won’t be happy about it,” Blake explained.

“But it doesn’t have to be this way. If you were to do an overall assessment of your life by making a list of everything you have going for you and everything against you, what would that list look like? What percent would be positive, and what percent would be negative? I’ve done this test with hundreds of people, and, generally speaking, most people would say their life is 85% positive and 15% negative. When they take into account where they live, the quality of our food, water, air, the freedoms we have, the healthcare system, protection from our enemies, and the general provisions for life that are available to us, the bottom line is we are in a pretty good place. I agree that there are things in our lives that are bad for every one of us. People get sick and die. People divorce each other or go bankrupt. Bad people take advantage of good people. There's a lot of junk out there. Still, when people assess and look at where they are compared to how it could be, most people would agree that life's pretty good—about 85% of it. So where do you want to live?" Blake asked.

"In the 85%!" answered Todd.

"Exactly," said Blake. "We want everyone to live in the 85%. If we choose to focus on better things, we will have a better environment. But it takes discipline. That's why when we do our 50/50 Meetings, we start by mapping out a game plan for people to be successes, not failures. We give them a prescription for success by showing them the four or five things they can do to be a total success. We are aware of the 15% to the extent that we are looking for anything that might prevent them from success. If we see someone is in a rough season, we know it's difficult for them to think about anything but the 15%, but our goal is to help them get out of that season and back into a positive place. That's one reason the **Business Goals** program taught us to do our 50/50 Meetings in a specific order—success in work first, a check to see if something is going on that might prevent that success (something negative), followed by a deliberate focus on the positive things going on in a person's life that we can continually celebrate with them.

"Experience shows that we encounter seasons less than 10% of the time. This means that for 90% of your One-on-Ones, you will talk about the positive things that people are doing in their lives—hobbies, families, community involvement, and the things in their life that are going well. It's important that we leave our One-on-Ones encouraging people to get back into the 85%. Even the people in bad seasons can be gently moved in that direction by pointing out the other positive areas of life. When people are in the darkest of despair, there is still something positive they can appreciate. We can always point people in the direction of hope. There may be times when it feels like everyone is in a season on your team. You need to move forward, look for positive things in the day, and provide hope for the future. You may go through a season yourself and need the support of your boss. It's often difficult to help the people on your team when you're knee-deep in a problem. If that happens, you need to let us help you through the season," Blake explained.

"I want to give you one other example of the 85/15 that is common in our relationships. When you met Sarah, you thought she was amazing, and you wanted to spend all your time with her. You naturally saw the great things about her that attracted you to her…the 85%. As time went by, you began to recognize a few things you weren't thrilled about with her. There was a 15%, but you chose to overlook those things, see only her positive 85%, and get married. Too many times, once we get married, we begin to focus on the 15%, and before we know it, that's all we can see. That's when many couples get divorced. What they don't realize is that the 85% is still there. The reasons they married the person haven't changed; they just changed their focus. When you re-focus on the 85%, everything moves back to the good, and relationships are restored," Blake told Todd.

"Todd, here's the bottom line. We will accomplish so much more and reach our goals and dreams if we maintain a positive attitude and live in the 85%...but it takes discipline. We must be deliberate about living in that 85%, both at work and home. I want you to do everything you can to live in the 85%. Make this your goal in everything situation you go into. Look for the positive and bring encouragement by looking at what's positive. Make it your goal to choose to live in the 85% starting right now. When you walk out of the office and go home today, think about how you will walk into your house tonight with a positive attitude focusing on what's going great. Don't listen to the news on the way home or anything that will get you back into the 15%. Instead, listen to something uplifting or nothing at all and just ponder the great things that are going on in your life and here at Severson."

Todd could tell this was one of the most important things to Blake.

He decided to be deliberate about living in the 85% from that moment on. He couldn't wait to see what effect it would have on him and the other people in his life.

CHAPTER SUMMARY

- If you did an assessment of everything positive in your life and everything negative, most people would say life is 85% positive and 15% negative.
- If there are challenging relationships in your life, is it because you are focusing only on the 15% in that relationship? You can change that by re-focusing on the 85%.
- The world leads us to live in the 15%. Nearly everything we hear is bad news or something negative.
- Choose to live in the 85% that is positive.

POINTS TO PONDER

- How would you assess your life? Is it close to 85% positive and 15% negative?
- Where have you been living—in the 85% or the 15%?
- Where have you been living relating to the relationships in your life, in the 85% or the 15%?
- Will you agree to start living in the 85%?

STEP FOUR

Living It Out

22

WORKING THE PROGRAM WITH CUSTOMERS, VENDORS, AND OTHERS

The following week, Todd and Blake met at their regular time. Blake wanted to know how things had gone after the past week's meeting. He was most interested in Todd's perspective on the last part of their conversation on attitude and focusing on the great things in our lives based on the successes and positive things in life. Blake wanted Todd to understand that a simple adjustment in how we think and what we allow to influence us will change our lives and everyone around us. Doing so will allow us to live more productive and happier lives. If we live a life based on hope and success instead of defeat and failure, the ensuing positive attitude will change our own lives and the lives of everyone around us.

"Todd, I'm hoping last week's discussion had a profound impact on you. Did you change anything or do anything different as a result of our discussion on the second half of the 50/50 Meeting and the importance of a positive attitude?" Blake asked.

"Well," Todd admitted, "I have to admit I've been living in the default mode most of my life. I tend to let the pressures of the day or the news or what the people around me complain about impact me...

negatively. My wife doesn't see it; I guess I don't let my grumpiness show outwardly, but I'm definitely not positive. I now recognize how that has hurt my wife, kids, and everyone I come in contact with. Ever since the day I left your office last week, I am starting to recognize my attitude. I'm now making a point to go into every meeting with a positive attitude. When I drive home, I try not to go into the house without thinking about being positive about my day and attitude. The best part of it is that I can see the instant and measurable impact. Everyone is different! They seem to mirror my demeanor. When I am more positive, they become more positive and have more of a bounce in their step. It's amazing what a huge difference and impact it has had on me and everyone around me.

"I also took to heart your comments about where I was focusing my attention in relationships, especially with Sarah. I think I tended to focus more on the 15% than I was on the great things about her. I started to recognize, each day, the great things about her and even told her why I appreciated her a few times. That made such a big difference in our relationship in just seconds. It was amazing. I'm so grateful for what you've shown me. I can't thank you enough," said Todd.

Todd's progress moved Blake. It isn't every day you get to see someone change for the better right before your eyes. But there was more to do. He wanted to show Todd how the program applied to their customers, vendors, and literally everyone he would come in contact with from here on out.

"You're welcome, Todd. I'm grateful for you too. Now let's talk about how the **Business Goals** program and the right side of the equation relate to our customers and vendors. You see, our customers have exactly the same long-term desires as our employees. They want to enjoy the people they work with, both in terms of their own employees and their vendors, and their customers. It all goes back to what's important in life and what people want. The same thing that employees want in the workplace applies to everyone, including our customers, our vendors, and even our families, which is why the **Business Goals** program teaches us right from the beginning to apply what we are learning to our families. Everyone wants to enjoy the people they are interacting with. Everyone wants and expects us to fulfill the contract. And everyone expects us to abide by a certain set of rules. So, if we know our customers want to enjoy the people they work with and, by extension, buy from, we can apply the program to them. All three steps can be applied.

"First, we need to understand their goals and objectives. What is it they need from us, and what are their expectations? This is fairly simple in our business. We sell products that people need for their cars. They can buy our products or someone else's. For most people, it starts with a price/quality/availability decision. Understanding that, we need to provide them with a product of good quality, guaranteed to be available when they need it, and at a cost that provides them with an adequate profit. Simple, right? What happens when our competitor shows up with the same solution? Their products offer the same price/quality/availability, and margin. The buyer has a choice. They will either try to get a better price or decide based on something else. I can tell you right now it will be the person they like the most—the one they enjoy doing business with. And my experience is that the people factor has more bearing on it than you might expect.

"I know people will sometimes give up price, quality, availability, or margin because they like the person and enjoy spending time with them. Therefore, starting with Step One is still important. You need to determine the top four or five things your customer wants to accomplish in priority order and the weight of each item. We also want to have a written set of goals for each customer. We'll ask the same questions you asked Sarah about being her dream husband, except we'll get them to name the top four or five things that would make us their dream supplier, prioritize them, and weigh them. Our goal is to meet our customer's needs, similar to how you meet your wife's needs. Doing that one thing already puts us one step ahead of our competition because they have never asked what the most important things are to the customer. Can you see how this works?" Blake asked.

"Definitely," Todd replied.

"Second, we need to make sure we have the right person in the right position for the client. The 5Cs are very important to them. Does our representative have the right Character, Competency, Chemistry, Capability, and Contribution for them? We want to assess this rather than assuming that the person we park in the position will be a good fit with each customer in that region. The component that is the most difficult to gauge is Chemistry. We have a pretty good idea when we put someone in the field that they have the other four Cs, but Chemistry is purely a personal fit. So we ask every salesman to assess their Chemistry with the client and then ask their supervisor to make a call from time to time on the client to make sure they are positive on all 5Cs, especially Chemistry. If we sense a problem, we bring in one or two of our other people to see if there might be a better fit. Customers will appreciate it when you move someone out who they have bad chemistry with.

"The other important component is to have the right strategy in place. We communicate clear expectations with the customer. What do they need from us by what date for them to feel we've succeeded? To a certain degree, we do the same thing with them but gently. We need them to know that to be successful in what we do, they need to maintain good communication with us. We also need to follow agreed-upon policies and procedures and make sure we get paid under the terms we agree to. Each time we meet with our customers, we make sure we agree to a new list of prioritized expectations. Often we will follow up a meeting with an email that memorializes what we discussed.

"As you may have guessed, we need to hold 50/50 Meetings with our customers as well. Sometimes these meetings will be Group 50/50s, but usually, they will be One-on-Ones. The group meetings will take the form of one of our salespeople meetings with a large group or a meeting with many people from both companies to discuss how the two firms will interact. We will follow the same format of making sure we discuss our goals and expectations first, which will comprise the first half of the meeting. Then we will take it upon ourselves to see how everyone is doing as a team. We usually ask them how their company is doing, inquire about any new initiatives, or perhaps discuss something we've heard about an employee and how we can encourage them. We essentially give them a testimony of how we work through similar situations in our company. There is always something we compliment them on so that we leave with a focus on the 85%," Blake explained.

"Most of our meetings with our customers will be One-on-Ones," continued Blake. "Again, we follow the same format. Goals and objectives first, followed by how we're doing as people. We do this from the very first time we meet them until the time they move on. My experience is that many salespeople understand the concept of a personal relationship, but they tend to make a mistake right off the bat by reversing the order. The order is key. You have to discuss the goals and objectives first, then the people."

"Why is this so important? Does it really make a difference which one we start with?" asked Todd.

"Yes, and here's why," explained Blake. "Everyone feels like they are the busiest person on earth. The last thing they have time for is a salesperson. If they give an appointment to a salesperson for some reason, that employee has about two minutes to say something that makes them want to keep listening. The customer will have no desire for a relationship with a person he never intends to buy from. So when a salesperson steps in and attempts to either break the ice or establish a personal relationship first, the customer usually stops listening and moves to end the meeting as quickly as possible. But we stick to our 50/50 plan. We understand the two-minute drill and want to make our point for doing business with us first. We typically start with, 'Thanks for taking the meeting. Let me get right to the point. We manufacture accessories for cars. Our prices are competitive, our quality is very good, and we deliver when we say we will deliver. What I believe sets us apart is that you will enjoy doing business with us. We have a specific set of rules we follow.' At this time, we either tell them our rules or hand them a business card that has the rules on the back. 'We want the opportunity to have you try our products and experience the service and support that comes with dealing with our company.' This usually leads to a variety of questions from the customer and allows us to show them how we seek to determine their top four or five needs and how we will meet those expectations. Usually, when the customer sees that we are different because we have a very specific system for determining their needs, we usually get a chance to bid," said Blake.

Blake could see it was making sense to Todd, so he continued. "Once the business objectives are completed, and it would appear that the meeting is done, then we move to the second half of the 50/50 Meeting. Even if it's on the way out and is not truly 50/50, we seek to know more about the person, then note the things in their office and ask about them. Most people will have a photograph of their family, hobby, or special interest. You just have to ask about it after you know they want to do business with you, and they will usually start talking. If they don't have anything obvious to ask about, you can ask them, 'So what do you do for fun?' It's a simple and innocuous question that can show you where their interests lie. It's also wise to tell them something about yourself that lets them know you are a person, not a machine. If they talk about their family, indicating that it is important to them, then you can tell them about your family. If they want to talk about their hobbies, you can tell them about your hobbies or learn more about them. It's actually fascinating to hear what people are passionate about. Then once you know what they're interested in, you'll know what to start the conversation with at your next 50/50 Meeting. If someone talks to you about their family, then next time, you can naturally ask how their family is doing after you've done the first part of the meeting."

Todd nodded. He had experienced that before with his Severson rep, and it did make a big difference to Todd that he remembered those details.

"We also know that our customers will go through the same good and bad seasons as our employees," said Blake. "So why wouldn't we want to do the same thing for them that we're willing to do for our employees? Customers will get sick, some will die, some will have babies, and some will get married. When you show concern and a desire to help them through their seasons, they will appreciate it. But get ready—you'll be setting a trend that nobody else is doing. Our society teaches the opposite. We are taught to pay attention only to ourselves and not look out for our friends, neighbors, acquaintances, or business associates. Severson Systems wants to treat them how we would like to be treated. We want to celebrate their good seasons with them and come to their assistance in difficult times. We've found the smallest things help tremendously. We've visited our customers in the hospital when they've had babies, car accidents, or serious illnesses. It's surprising to them that you would care enough to visit them. In fact, the first time I visited a customer in the hospital, they were shocked. They couldn't believe I actually came to see them with care and concern. And the moment they determine that I sincerely care, it's a whole new ballgame. They will go out of their way to help you succeed at what you're doing.

"Admittedly, you may have to go just to help build the relationship, but as time goes by, I think you'll enjoy helping or celebrating with them far more than the future financial successes that come from it. That's why I told you when we first met that we are about more than money and climbing ladders. What happens in the process is that you will also be meeting your number one need. Your number one desire is to enjoy the people you work with, including customers, and when that need is met in a natural and deep way, that payoff becomes far more important than the money. Don't make the mistake of saying you don't want to bother them in their time of trouble or joy. People appreciate those who show them genuine interest, care, and concern. Yet many mistakenly take the attitude that they should not visit the hospital because they do not have an invitation. It doesn't occur to the patient to extend an invitation to their representative from Severson, whom they barely know, to come to visit them. They don't want to impose on your life, and it wouldn't even hit their radar screen during whatever turmoil or joy they are in the hospital for. Your visit can be short and sweet. 'I just wanted to stop by and bring you flowers and cookies and see if there was anything I could do for you.' As with the employee, just asking that question is huge."

IT'S THE SAME WITH VENDORS

"Okay, I've gone over the program with customers. Now let's talk for just a moment about our vendors—the people we buy goods and services from. We do the same thing with them. In any meeting, we can dictate how it goes. When someone attempts to sell something to us for the first time, we ask that they get right to the point and explain why we should do business with them. I usually ask them to give me their thirty-second elevator speech on what they do and why anyone should use their goods or services. I'm always surprised at how many people don't have a well-prepared thirty-second elevator pitch. If it's not compelling, and I think we have what they are offering covered very well somewhere else, I'll save them time and my time, too. I'll politely excuse them and thank them for stopping by. If they say something compelling that piques my interest, I will give them my top four or five priorities for potentially buying their product or service and what I expect of them to get my business. Then once we've gone through the goals and expectations, I will start a 50/50 Meeting with them. I want to know something about them, how and why they work for the company they work for, their hobbies, and how they spend their spare time. In that process, I'm forming an opinion about whether I like them, how they score on the 5Cs, and if I would like to work with them, regardless of what their proposal looks like. When they come back, I'll have made a note about what we talked about, and we will start forming a relationship. If something happens in their life, we show them the same support that we do with our employees and customers. In doing this, we've built solid relationships with our vendors, many of whom have stepped up to the plate in a big way to help us when we've needed it. They've helped us get a special price when we needed to be more competitive. They've gone out of their way to meet a delivery deadline when it didn't seem possible, and they've even introduced us to people when we are looking for employees. They even introduced us to new clients! Many vendors have become our best recruiters for our company for new hires because they know everyone in the industry; they know the great employees at other companies and how great it is to work at Severson. Both companies have benefited because we truly enjoy working with each other," Blake explained.

It all made such good sense to Todd, yet he had never really thought about it in this way.

THE FRIENDS AND FAMILY PLAN

"I think you understand that the **Business Goals** program works in all aspects of life. We spent a lot of time talking about how it works for our employees, but then I showed you how it works for our customers and vendors. And, throughout the **Business Goals** course, you were told to practice the concepts from the program at home in addition to the office. We talked a lot about how things went when you deployed the concepts at home in our weekly meetings. The bottom line is that the program provides the essential components necessary to have a relationship with anyone. But the most important relationships we have in life are our families.

"I hope you use the plan at home, Todd. Set goals with your wife and kids and learn what they would like to accomplish for the next year. Then get their lists of four or five things that would make you their dream dad and dream husband. Meet with them regularly and give them the attention they want and need. We've had many people who thought their relationships were too far gone with their wives and kids even to begin doing these drills. Yet when an effort was made to improve things, and both parties recognized that it would be better to work through the tough stuff rather than throw in the towel, the payoff was great," said Blake.

Blake leaned in and said, "I'm not sure if you've had a great marriage for all the years you've been married, but if your goal is for it to grow and thrive, this program works. When you show Sarah that you take her list seriously and incorporate her needs into your daily activity, she will appreciate it. Do the 50/50 Meetings with Sarah and your kids. Unless you actually meet and spend time with them, you can't possibly be meeting their needs."

On the outside, Todd was fine. He nodded and gave the appearance that everything was great. But on the inside, he was hurting. He thought about his marriage and all the lost time with his kids and wife. All that energy that they'd spent on stuff that doesn't matter and isn't important. His kids are almost grown and out of the house, and his marriage has some deep scars. Had he thought about meeting with his wife and kids each year and making goals for the family or gotten a list of the top four or five needs for his wife and kids and spent some one-on-one time each week with each of them—things would be very different now. *Much different.*

Blake sensed Todd's unease and asked what he was thinking. He knew it was likely Todd had some of the problems that occur in families when you don't have a program like this, so he said, "You know, Todd, the good thing about this program is that it's never too late to start. You may have some remorse for not knowing about the **Business Goals** before, but you now have a choice. You can either embrace the program and begin to implement it into your life, or you can go on with the way things are."

Though Todd didn't feel much better, it did make sense. He knew he had to implement the program in his personal life and professional life. He knew deep down inside things would improve. They already had improved in a measurable way at home. As Blake walked Todd to his door that week, he encouraged him to implement every aspect of the program at work and home and remain focused on the positive things in his life.

At that moment, Todd made a personal commitment to do just that.

CHAPTER SUMMARY

- One-on-Ones are important with everyone in your life—customers, vendors, employees, and family members.
- The **Business Goals** program and the right side of the equation apply to our customers, vendors, and everyone we contact, including our friends and family.
- People will decide who to do business with based on whom they like best if all other things are equal.
- If you ask the people around you what's important to them in what order and with what weight, they will normally tell you. Then you simply have to live up to their expectation.

- The order for the customer 50/50 Meeting is just as important as with the employee 50/50 Meeting.
    - Define success relating to work first.
    - Discuss the personal side of life second.
- When meeting someone in business for the first time, don't waste their time. Get right to the point.
    - Determine the top four or five most important things to your customer or vendor.
    - Put them in priority order and give them weight. Nobody else does this.
- Customers and vendors will go through the same seasons, good and bad, just as you and your employees will. You can help them through their seasons, too.
- Don't be afraid to lead people into a 50/50 Meeting when they want to do business or get to know you.
- Ask vendors to tell you why you need to do business with them in thirty seconds or less.
- Prioritize what will make them successful in working with you and give weight to each item.

POINTS TO PONDER

- Will you consider the 50/50 Meeting with everyone you come in contact with?
- Do you waste people's time by trying to establish a relationship first?
    - Can you reverse the order and see if there's a reason to do business with each other first?
- As your customers and vendors go through seasons, will you help them just as you would someone in your family?

23

DEPLOYING THE PROGRAM COMPANYWIDE

Todd was down to the final details of learning how Severson deploys the **Business Goals** program. But learning it and deploying it were two different things just as teaching the fundamentals of golf and playing golf are different. The first few swings can be pretty funny.

"Todd, today I want to explain how we've deployed the **Business Goals** program throughout our company. We use the same deployment process the **Business Goals** program teaches. First, the top person in each division, team, or company must learn and agree to deploy the program. Then that person teaches it to their direct reports. Their direct reports learn and practice the program with their supervisor and then teach it to the people who report to them, and so on. Essentially, one level teaches it to the next level and then the next level until the entire company has implemented the program. We encourage everyone to attend the **Business Goals** in-person classes just as you did, Todd. If that's not practical, they can watch self-paced videos, or their supervisor can teach them. Once they complete the first six weeks of learning the program, we continue living out the program every week. Here's a copy of the annual calendar; you can see how this works throughout the year," said Blake.

ANNUAL CALENDAR

Week 1	Introduction and overview of the program
Week 2	Define and refine your personal and company goals
Week 3	Determine the right people in the right position
Week 4	Define your rules and core values
Week 5	Define 4–5 most important things to accomplish (by weight and priority)
Week 6	Deploy the 50/50 Meeting
Week 7	Complete the Windfall Test with your team
Week 8	Complete 5Cs assessments on team
Week 10	Complete 85/15 on team
Week 12	Deploy the Business Goals app
Week 14	New quarterly goals: team alignment
Week 16	Reality check: what's working/what's not
Week 18	Calibrate with spouse/children/team leaders
Week 20	Review rules/relationships/responsibilities
Week 22	Quarterly Reviews: simple using the app
Week 24	Quarterly planning: what needs work
Week 26	New quarterly goals: team alignment (do 85/15)
Week 28	Reality check: what's working/what's not
Week 30	Calibrate with spouse/children/team leaders
Week 32	Review rules/relationships/responsibilities
Week 34	Quarterly reviews: simple using the app
Week 36	Quarterly planning: what needs work
Week 38	New quarterly goals: team alignment
Week 40	Reality check: what's working/what's not
Week 42	Calibrate with spouse/children/team leaders
Week 44	Review rules/relationships/responsibilities
Week 46	Quarterly reviews: simple using the app
Week 48	Quarterly planning: what needs work
Week 50	New annual goals: team alignment
Week 52	Prepare to launch into the next year

Blake said, "As you can see, we look at our year in terms of weeks, months, and quarters. This calendar is a roadmap for individual and group meetings. The calendar also incorporates a check and balance system into the program. So far, you know the program requires weekly meetings where you calibrate expectations with your employees. Our annual calendar adds another layer of responsibility. It's a system to check and reevaluate how things are going, especially as it relates to our corporate goals. At week twelve, we ask everyone to revise their quarterly goals based on what's working well and what's not. Halfway into every new quarter, we want you to do an assessment of how things are going with your team—you'll see that in week sixteen. Then every quarter, we want to remind everyone to keep putting an effort toward the home front. We do that by encouraging employees to reassess their goals with their families and the people in the office. Finally, we ask everyone to review the rules and core values regularly. We've found that when we discuss our rules and core values weekly and hold quarterly meetings to talk about how everything is going, we tend to live them out better. Most companies have strategic plans or business plans. Few have annual calendars that hold them accountable for achieving their goals or plans. I firmly believe that if you want to be successful, you need the discipline to hold you to it. Otherwise, it tends to be forgotten.

"The calendar also helps with our strategic planning. At the beginning of the year, we set annual goals. Each person then sets their goals for the year in alignment with our corporate goals. Each member of the team should be able to explain their contribution to the big picture and why the company may not be able to reach the annual goal without them.

"It may take a week or two for a division or company to go through the process of determining what their goals are for the year," said Blake. "For example, each year, we hire outside consultants to help us develop strategic plans and annual goals. That process takes a few weeks because we get input from key people on the management team and then integrate that into the consultant's process. Once we complete that process, we can plug those strategic and annual goals right into the **Business Goals** app to complete Step One. Next, it takes a few weeks for a manager to work through the process of who he will need to fulfill the strategic plan. Remember, they need to be able to support and defend why each person is on the team and how he wouldn't be able to meet the annual plan if they weren't on the team. That may be a culture change for many companies that plug bodies into positions instead of knowing the strengths and weaknesses of each person on the team. It can really take the steam out of a team when people are plugged in who are incompetent or are put into a position simply because they have been there for years. Instead, employees should be reassigned into positions where they can add value by accomplishing something of value for the organization. When you put the wrong person into a position, it becomes difficult for others to succeed because those who aren't accomplishing anything for the team can bring the whole team down. This also happens when a company puts a favored relative into a position that really can't do the job. It is common in municipalities or government posts where people are tenured into positions but have stopped working for practical purposes. That's the person who simply has run out of gas but needs pay and somehow feels entitled to keep working because of the many prior years of faithful service. They forgot that they were already paid for those years, and they are not entitled to an extended payout.

"Todd, there's one other interesting thing we've learned about the program relating to its deployment—it can be forced one level up and all levels down. We heard about this in the **Business Goals** class, and then we witnessed it with one of our contractors. We had someone from another company work in our factory as an outside contractor for an extended period. In that process, they were taught the program by our staff members. They went back to their own company and asked to implement the **Business Goals** program. The owners didn't want to deploy the program for whatever reason, so the supervisor did it anyway within his department. In that process, he had no problem making his boss participate in the program. He simply started by defining his goals and then went through the same process to ensure he had the right team with defined weekly responsibilities by priority and weight. Then they started weekly or bi-weekly One-on-One 50/50 Meetings with his team and his boss and found a way to incorporate some rules. That department of the company consistently had the highest performance and income, and the owner really liked the way the supervisor was running the department. Eventually, the supervisor was able to deploy the program companywide. So, it works even if people won't formally adopt the program. I'm telling you this because you may explain the program to a vendor or even your wife, and they may choose to implement it where they work," said Blake.

JUNIORS, ACCOUNTABILITY PARTNERS, AND BEST FRIENDS

"There's one other topic I'd like to cover today about three specific management initiatives we use here at Severson that you need to know about. One is the Junior Program, another is the Accountability Partner Program, and the third is the Best Friend Program.

"Let's start with the Junior Program. I know you're a sports fan and understand the concept of first-string, second-string, etc. This is essentially the Junior Program. Who is on the bench that could instantly move into your spot if you are injured, on vacation, or taken out completely? It's your junior—the person on the bench for you. Here at Severson, we want every person to have a junior in training capable of running onto the field for them so the company doesn't miss a beat. We may not perform as well with the junior, but we won't lose the game," Blake explained.

"In professional sports, this concept is done very well. Take basketball, for instance. There are five starters on a basketball team. Those five starters rarely play the entire game. They are taken out for rest periods or because they have too many fouls. When they come out, nobody thinks twice when their junior runs onto the court and picks up where they left off. That's how we want it here. We want everyone inside and outside the company to be aware of our Junior Program and who the junior is for each person. It shouldn't even be a concern when they see the junior filling in for their senior. The senior must either be on vacation, take a day off, be out sick, or do something else.

"When we first started this program, we didn't have enough depth to have a junior for every person. So there were juniors for multiple people. I was the junior for our sales, production, and purchasing managers. Then as we grew, we found we could bring people up from within the ranks and begin to teach them the fundamentals of their boss's job.

"There were several unexpected bonuses that came out of this program. It became a very low-cost promotion system. For someone to be named the junior to their boss was a promotion of sorts, but it didn't have to come with a pay increase. We found that we were feeding an employee's desire for intellectual stimulation when we named them a junior and began a training process. Another bonus we hadn't anticipated was the performance and increased productivity component. When employees were asked to train someone as their junior, they improved at their job. The 'two heads are better than one' motto really began to mean something as the senior and junior on the team started performing at a much higher rate. The junior challenged why certain things were done, and our processes improved. The senior person got better because they were constantly being watched and had to be deliberate about what they were teaching and doing. It's a terrific system," boasted Blake.

"So let me explain how we began and then maintained this system. First, we agreed as a company that we would adopt the Junior Program. We announced to the employees that we were putting the Junior Program in place and that every employee would be training a junior, no matter how new or low they were on the totem pole. Next, we explained that this system is important because we never know when someone might be out sick, have an accident, or leave for whatever reason. We explained that it makes sense so we can cover for people who need time off for vacations or attend to personal business. Everyone thought it made good sense, and nearly everyone was happy to participate. Only a few people didn't want to name or train their junior because the company would find out about their poor job performance. We put the Junior Program in when we launched the **Business Goals** program. It turns out, we would have found out about the poor performance with our 50/50 Meetings anyway. We replaced a few people when we learned about their performance and reluctance to name their Junior. We probably would have just kept putting up with their poor performance had we not initiated the **Business Goals** and the Junior concepts. On a more positive note, our overall morale and productivity increased dramatically from implementing both programs," Blake explained.

"Okay, back to implementing and maintaining the system. Once you've announced the program and everyone understands the reason for it, the next step is for each person to name their junior and be able to support and defend why they chose that person. People need to choose a junior who can actually do their job and make a contribution to the position, not just fill the space with a body. Sometimes people will try to pick someone significantly underqualified for the position so they look better. That doesn't fly. Make sure your employees know the person they pick will be a reflection on them and their department. If they pick people who are not competent, it will certainly reflect on the senior. We heard a saying that Steve Jobs said that played out in this process, 'A-players hire A-players, and B-players hire C-players.'[4] Once we told people the saying, everyone tried their best to pick someone they thought could equal or better their own performance. We explained it wasn't a risk to their position so much as a reflection on their management ability and self-confidence.

"Next, the employee needed to set up a training schedule and curriculum. The schedules should be set so they don't conflict with peak performance times. The curriculum should be simple enough to be understood and complete enough to get the job done. Every employee's senior should review the schedule and curriculum to make sure it makes sense and that the job is being done. The training curriculum is a fairly easy process. The senior can use their goals, job description, and expectations as the framework and then fill in the details of how they accomplish it. Another bonus to the Junior Program is that you typically get your processes down on paper. The **Business Goals** app came in very handy because it had in writing what everyone was doing," Blake explained.

"Do you have a junior?" Todd asked.

"Of course I do," Blake responded. "He's our Vice President of Operations, Kevin Simpson. I feel very confident that if something

---

[4] "What's An A-Player?" Dr. Jim Walsh, CTO, GlobalLogic.com, last accessed March 25, 2022; https://www.globallogic.com/insights/blogs/whats-an-a-player/#:~:text=Steve%20Jobs%20used%20to%20say,most%20senior%2C%20regardless%20of%20role.

happened to me, he could easily run the ship until the company could be transitioned," Blake said.

"Finally," concluded Blake, "we have the juniors shadow their seniors regularly and even fill in for them from time to time even when the senior isn't away from the job. This builds the confidence necessary and helps the rest of the staff, our vendors, and our customers become comfortable with the junior. We want to make it so seamless that if we see a junior in place, we don't think anything of it on any given day. We review the junior's abilities and performance on a quarterly and annual basis through the scoring system we talked about."

ACCOUNTABILITY PARTNERS

"The next program I want you to know about is our Accountability Partner Program. We decided we needed an accountability system because we are dedicated to our rules and core values. We set up employees in teams of two as accountability partners. We allow the employees to choose their accountability partners. There are a variety of reasons we need this program. First, I figured out the hard way that we all have blind spots. Remember I told you about first starting this program and asking some of my employees for feedback? I had several blind spots. I didn't see the impact some of my actions or statements had on others around me. As you might know, there's almost no accountability for CEOs in the business world. The ongoing **Business Goals Intensive** program that I belong to has really helped me as I meet with two other CEOs every month. It also helped me set up the accountability partner system here so everyone can have a second set of eyes and ears looking out for them. We often say things that we mean one way, but people interpret them differently. The accountability program is designed to have someone close to you that can tell you something without the fear that it might be taken the wrong way. Accountability partners have permission, under the company's guidelines, to communicate with you what they hear or see you doing. If they suspect something you do or say could be misinterpreted, they can bring it up to you so you can fix it before it does any damage. The accountability partner can also watch what you're doing and look out for you relating to the rules and core values. If we all agree that we want to live up to the rules and core values, then sometimes we will need someone to hold us accountable to those rules and core values. Sometimes we don't realize we are breaking one or more of the rules, and we need that accountability partner to bring it to our attention. In the beginning, it's tough to allow accountability into your life, but I can tell you that sometimes we just need a little help along the way. The Accountability Partner Program provides that help. It's also in line with our desire to seek feedback, as we discussed earlier.

"Now, let me go over how we initiate it and keep it going. As with the Junior Program, we started with an announcement. We explained that we wanted employees to find another person to be their accountability partner and provide feedback. Then we asked that they meet bi-weekly to check in with one another. Each agrees to be the second set of eyes and ears for the other and watches out for them and listens to and watches their behavior. If they see something inconsistent with our rules, core values, or job performance issues, they can bring it up. Obviously, it helps to pick an accountability partner in your same department or who has a similar job. It doesn't work to pick someone who is a subordinate, as they may not feel they have the authority to say anything. We invite every member of our company to speak to anyone at any level when it comes to accountability and our rules or core values, however," Blake explained.

"There have been some real benefits from the accountability program. First, when an employee's performance changes and we suspect a problem or potential season, one of the first people we go to is their accountability partner. Second, the accountability partner system has allowed employees to form a deeper relationship with someone at work. It is one more building block to establish and create an environment where people can enjoy the people they work with. Finally, when someone is in a season, the accountability partner usually becomes the primary liaison between the person in the season and the company. For most people, their accountability partner becomes a trusted friend. He or she becomes part of a support mechanism. It's a very valuable system," Blake said with confidence. "I've written one of our Value Discussions on the topic of accountability. I thought you'd like to see it, so I printed a copy."

Severson Systems

Who Are You Accountable To?

Have you ever said, "I wish someone had told me before I made that bad decision?" Or, have you ever known you were walking down a path that was wrong but just didn't have anyone to talk to? It happens to all of us. There is a solution—an Accountability Partner.

Nine times out of ten, you will take the right course of action if you know you have someone to answer to about your decision. Have you heard about the "Announcement Test"? It works like this: If you announced your intentions to 100 people of high moral character, would they support your decision? Chances are, occasionally they would not support your decision.

For example, your employer makes a mistake on your paycheck in your favor. Do you keep the money? Without the Announcement Test, you might rationalize the mistake and say, "The company can afford it," or "They must have wanted me to have this money." Bottom line is that it's a simple mistake and comes out of your employer's pocket. If you announced your intentions to the 100 people of high moral character, all of them would tell you to report the mistake to the company and let them decide what should be done.

Here's why this is so important. We all have fairly similar rules and core values. We all demand honesty of each other. We would like loyalty from everyone we know (friends, customers, spouses, vendors, etc.). Nobody wants to be cheated or stolen from. Everyone wants respect. We all want these things, yet sometimes we don't always give them in return. Sometimes we stumble and violate one of those same values that we expect from everyone else.

That's where the Announcement Test and the Accountability Partner come in. If you knew that you had to run every decision past 100 people of the highest character and your accountability partner, you may make some different decisions. You wouldn't have been rude to the person who cut you off or pushed in front of you. You wouldn't keep the extra change you get by mistake, and you would never lie.

While it's impossible to think you could actually announce every thought or every action to 100 people, it is possible to consider just one person: your Accountability Partner. This is someone who is not your spouse or significant other, but rather someone of the same sex who can and will hold you truly accountable for all your actions. Make it a two-way street.

Hold your partner accountable for his or her own actions as well.

Try it. Pick someone you can trust—someone to whom you would entrust your life savings or a life-or-death decision. Ask that person to become your Accountability Partner. Explain that you would like to meet regularly to tell each other what's going on in your lives. Explain that the goal is to help each other make the right decisions and choices. Good, honest, and moral decisions. The same ones that conform to how you want to be treated by others.

For most people, this is a very difficult step. It's hard to have someone hold you accountable, especially when doing the right thing is harder than doing the wrong thing. However, difficult steps lead to the greatest accomplishments and changes in your life. Give it a try.

YOUR BEST FRIEND

"The last thing I want to talk to you about today, Todd, is our Best Friend Initiative. As we've grown, we've said we want to grow with employees just like the ones already here. We like our employees, and they are doing a great job for us. We want our employees to feel this is the best place to work—the kind of place they wish all their friends could work. So we simply formalized that idea. We put a lot of time and energy into choosing our employees, and we've found that most of their friends are very similar to them. So we started a system in which we've asked every employee to make a list of two or three friends they can't wait to come on board. We then ask them to invite those friends to the plant from time to time, so they know who we are and vice versa. Sometimes they'll just stop by during a coffee break, and other times our employees will bring them over on their day off. As we've needed people, we go to our employees in similar positions and ask them to see if the people on their list might be available for an interview. Because this is a formal program, our employees usually tell their friends that they are on their list, and they hope that someday they will work at Severson. We've had outstanding success with this system since we hire people who usually rate fairly high with the 5Cs. It's been especially effective in our production areas. Admittedly, it's more difficult at the senior management levels but still effective. In fact, you were on our Sales Manager's list for quite some time. We gave you a call when the need materialized and set up that fateful lunch. If you think about it, we could easily double the size of our company with little difficulty if we called everyone on every employee's list. It can get pretty tough to find good employees, but this system works.

"So, Todd, I want you to do three things as a result of today's meeting. First, think about your junior. Which team member will you choose that makes the most sense, that you can support and defend in the position, and that will do a great job if you're not here? Second, I want you to pick an accountability partner. I would suggest one of your peers who is another regional manager. One last comment on that. Don't pick a woman. We don't like to team up with people of the opposite sex as accountability partners because we don't want to create a scenario for two people to become more than teammates. Third, I want you to make a list of two or three people you would love to have working here."

Todd instantly thought about both Brian and Grant. Grant could do the same job he was doing, and Brian could work somewhere in the plant. That was an obvious choice for him.

QUARTERLY SCORECARDS

"The final thing we need to go over is our scoring system. As you learned in the **Business Goals** class, people will do what they are inspected to do, not what they are expected to do. It's why they created the **Business Goals** app. It's a simple tool that allows us to instantly see where people stand in terms of completing their top three to four priorities each week."

People will do what they are inspected to do, not what they are expected to do.

Blake went on. "Now, let me explain how it works. It's a very objective system, and people score themselves. You'll remember from one of our earlier sessions that people fire themselves. That's because they score themselves and determine their own consequences. Here's how it works. Each week everyone lists their accomplishments for that week. The app then allows them to track their progress and report, by percentage, how much they've completed. We agree in advance that the target is 80% or better. A score of 70% puts someone on the radar screen as an under-performer; you'll remember that term from the **Business Goals** class. A score of 90% or better makes them a high achiever, which is great. When you look at a list of priorities for anyone using the app, each priority is color-coded according to their level of achievement. Better than 80% puts them in the green; 70% to 79% puts them in the yellow, and below 69% puts them in the red. Both the employee and the supervisor can instantly see if people are in the red, yellow, or green. It provides everyone with instant feedback and forms the basis for discussion during our weekly 50/50 Meetings where we align expectations," Blake told Todd.

Blake had his phone out and showed Todd the red, yellow, and green scores for someone on Todd's team. Todd had seen the color-coded scoring and understood it from the **Business Goals** class but was now reminded how important this was in tracking performance and helping every employee instantly know where they stand.

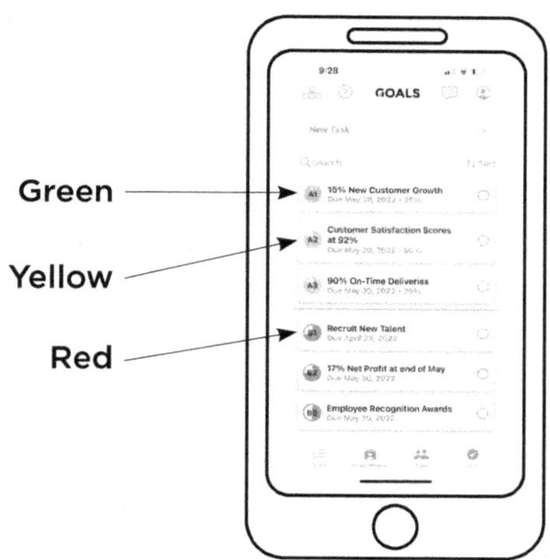

"You'll remember from the top five things people want in the workplace, recognition for your job was the fourth most important thing people wanted. There are a few components to the **Business Goals** app that accomplishes this. First, when someone completes a task, it gives them some instant recognition for doing a great job, and fireworks go off in the background. It may seem silly, but it lets them know they've won at completing a task. Second, when people see they are in the green, they have a sense of peace that they are doing what's expected of them—they are fulfilling the contract. Finally, the app notifies the supervisor when a task is completed. This allows the supervisor to be a great coach and give the employee an "atta-boy" or "atta-girl" for completing a priority. People here almost always run in the green. We set realistic 80% levels that everyone can achieve and encourage them to strive for 90% or better, plus we make a big deal about it when they do.

"The system also provides a great platform for ongoing performance evaluations and promotions. As you saw in our annual calendar, we do quarterly reviews. We simply keep track of where each person stood each week. The **Business Goals** desktop version of the app keeps a record of 'completed tasks' to easily see everyone's list of accomplishments. If you haven't seen that part of the **Business Goals** app, Todd, go to **app.businessgoals.org**. The system allows us to see where people stand in overall achievement and provides a window into whether someone should be promoted and given more responsibility," said Blake.

"Todd," said Blake, "we've followed the **Business Goals** program here for years, and here's what I've learned from it. When we put in place goals that point to our overarching goal to become everyone's favorite company and each person is aware of their personal goals, and we follow that by ensuring every person on our team is the right person in the right seat, and we follow that by doing the four or five most important things every day, by priority and weight, and we weigh the decisions we make through the **CAP** test and/or the Eight Tests, hold our 50/50 Meetings, and apply this to everyone we come in contact with, that's when life changes in an amazing way. It may seem like a lot, but when you break it down and do little bits each day, it becomes part of our routine. The result is that people enjoy working here, and we have satisfied customers, vendors, and great families. I hope you find that to be true for you as well."

"There's one other thing. When we follow the **Business Goals** program, we reach our goals…and that's something only 8% of people who set goals achieve—and that's pretty cool," Blake concluded.

Todd couldn't help but feel that he had really accomplished something of great value. He had that strong sense of enjoyment that comes with completing something big. The **Business Goals** program he had learned was huge, and he thanked Blake for spending so much time with him over the past several months. He was so happy to be part of the company and knew it would be one of the most important decisions of his life, all because of a simple program called **Business Goals**. There was just one more piece, and he would be done...or so he thought.

CHAPTER SUMMARY

- The program must be adopted and embraced by those who implement it.
    - — The program can be forced one level up and all levels down.
- People can learn about the **Business Goals** program by attending live classes, watching the video series, or from others who have gone through it before them.
- Most companies and individuals fall short of their goals because they don't have anything that helps them deploy their plans throughout the year.
    - — The **Business Goals** program calendar and the app provide the discipline a company needs to achieve its goals.
- Everyone in the company should have an understudy. We call it your junior.
    - — This is someone trained to do the other's job if they are on vacation, sick, or leave for any reason.
- The Junior Program improves productivity.
    - — Employees and systems will improve as one person trains another.
    - — It is the answer for the company to continue during any season.
    - — Job description, priorities, and goals can be used as the training curriculum.
- Everyone needs accountability.

We recommend implementing an Accountability Partner Program at all levels, especially the CEO level. CEOs may want to consider the **Business Goals Intensive** program.

- If you like your employees, you would probably like their friends. Their friends might make good employees—the Best Friend Initiative.
- The Best Friend Initiative asks every employee to make a list of friends they would like to see come and work with them.
- The Best Friend Initiative allows you to double the size of your company very quickly.
- Throughout school, you are given quarterly report cards. The **Business Goals** app allows every employee to know how they are doing in real-time.
- Follow the **Business Goals** program, and you can reach your goals, something only 8% of those who set written goals achieve.

POINTS TO PONDER

- Will you teach the **Business Goals** program to those who report to you?
- Will you follow the plan by using the **Business Goals** app to implement the annual calendar?
- Do you have a junior?
    - Are they capable of doing your job?
- Do you have an accountability partner?
- Which of your friends would you like to see come and work with you?
- Do you have a quarterly scoring or review system?
- Have you consistently achieved the goals you've put in place?

24

GRADUATION

It had been several months since Todd had started with Severson Systems. He was implementing each of the prior week's sessions with his team and family. He had even brought Grant up to speed on most of what he had learned and told him he was someone who should consider working at Severson too. Todd's life had changed dramatically. He now understood why he had joined Severson Systems and what was different about the company.

Todd focused on the things that mattered most—his family and friends first and then the people he worked with. He was working with a deliberate purpose and plan. He had goals at home and the office. He was setting weekly objectives with expectations. He held 50/50 Meetings with the individuals on his team, with customers and vendors, and with his wife and kids. He was in a supportive environment for the first time in his life. He had never known what that looked like before. And he was more interested in what was happening with the people at work, at home, and with his friends than with his golf clubs, his motorcycle, and any of his other possessions. He learned that possessions could be used as tools to help build relationships instead of fueling his own selfish desires. Now he understood the connection he needed to have with his kids, and he was making it happen. And for the first time in many years, he and his wife focused on each other's needs and enjoyed each other. He honestly loved his wife more now than he could ever remember.

Blake hadn't told Todd anything he hadn't heard before. He had heard almost everything he learned from the **Business Goals** class and Blake in bits and pieces throughout his life. What made it different was the way it was packaged. It was a specific program that incorporated all of these important components into one easily defined and easily followed plan.

The following week, Todd dropped by Blake's office at the normal time that they had been meeting. He wanted to tell Blake that it felt strange not to meet with him. His life had changed dramatically in a short amount of time, and he had Blake to thank. He felt more joy and happiness because he was focusing on the things that mattered most in life. In addition, he was working in a place that recognized this and modeled it.

Blake told Todd that afternoon that the process hadn't ended, instead had just begun. Now it was up to Todd to live it out. As they talked about the program, Blake gave Todd yet another piece of advice about the **Business Goals** program and the right side of the equation.

"Todd, the program you've learned can be taught to anyone. It's not just for you and me; it's for everyone. The **Business Goals** program teaches people to fulfill their primary needs and desires in life," said Blake. "I encourage you to tell your friends about it and other people you meet. Practice it daily, and you can live a fulfilled life with purpose."

That comment made Todd think back to the three most important things in his life. He remembered Blake had a different number one item on his list. It was his faith. Todd asked Blake, "You told me you would tell me about the number one item on your list sometime. I'd like to hear about that." Maybe there was something to it that Todd needed to hear about. After all, it seemed to be a big part of Blake's life.

Blake was overjoyed. He genuinely cared about Todd and knew faith could play an important part in his life. "I'd be happy to tell you about the role that my faith plays in my life. Why don't we set up a few weekly meetings on Friday afternoons?"

CHAPTER SUMMARY

- The **Business Goals** program has components you've probably been aware of your whole life, but it is packaged to allow you to focus on the most important things.
- Setting goals is important. Only 8% of people set goals and achieve them. That's why they are successful.
- Goals won't materialize without the involvement of people.
- Pursuing, pleasing, and meeting the needs of people in your life will bring the best results.
- Focus on the things that matter most in life.

POINTS TO PONDER

- There are three steps to the **Business Goals** program:
    1. Set goals
    2. Put the right people in the right seat to accomplish your goals
    3. Deploy the program weekly using the 50/50 Meeting
- During the deployment phase, use the 50/50 Meeting to incorporate your rules and core values.
- Will you deploy these three steps?
- Will you seek to pursue, please, and meet the needs of all the people around you?
- Will you focus on the three things that matter most in your life?

25

BECOMING RELATIONALLY CONSCIOUS

Read a book on flying, and you'll learn the rules, methods, language, and physics of flying. You may completely understand every aspect of how a plane flies. You may even be able to get a plane off the ground and land it. But you won't master flying until you gain the experience by logging in many hours of practice with someone coaching you through the process.

The same is true of the **Business Goals** program. The **Business Goals** program and the right side of the equation will not happen the instant you complete this book. I have provided steps, tools, and processes you can use, but now you must practice them. I strongly recommend you attend a **Business Goals** class. Classes are taught online, and you can go to businessgoals.org to find a class that fits your schedule.

I'm confident that when you implement what you've read in this book or attend a class, there will be an immediate payoff. You will begin to fulfill your goals and the most important things in your life.

Do you want better relationships with those around you and the people you love? Do you want to enjoy your work environment? Would you like contentment in your career, knowing you're achieving your goals while at the same time forming lifelong relationships? These are rhetorical questions. Focus on the **Business Goals** program and the right side of the equation, and your answers to these questions will materialize.

We've learned one other significant thing by deploying the **Business Goals** program and the right side of the equation. The right side validates the left side. By determining the most important things to work on that meet the needs and please those around us, at work and home, we form better relationships with them. You'll remember that Blake asked his wife for a list that would make him her dream husband (and allow him to fulfill the contract from her point of view). He wanted to be her dream husband so they would have the best possible relationship—so she would enjoy being with him. Fulfilling the contract (left side of the equation) is crucial for enjoying the people you're with (right side of the equation). These are the top two things people want in the workplace and at home.

Our story ended with Todd asking Blake about his faith in the previous chapter. There's a faith component to this program, which I believe is why it works 100% of the time. Whether you believe in God and the Bible is your own decision—it's called free will. However, if you did a quick study of the Bible and asked, "What is the most important thing to God or message of the Bible?" you would find the answer is two simple things: love God and love people. A simple study would tell you that loving God is all about living a life by the Ten Commandments (rules). Loving people is about pursuing, pleasing, and meeting the needs of others. Fulfilling the contract and enjoying the people around you is entirely about loving people. Putting rules in your life will almost always align with the Ten Commandments.

Isn't it interesting that the top three things everyone in the world wants, crossing all cultures and all religions, are also the most important things to God? Building a life around what God and people want will produce great results (and doing something that pleases God may also come with some advantages, whether you believe He exists or not). Don't believe God exists or choose not to pay attention to His existence or the

Bible? No problem, the program still works. But maybe there's a connection there you should investigate deeper…

Here's a recap of the program:

STEP ONE:
Write down your goals.

a. Create an overarching goal first, like "Winning the Super Bowl."
b. Create the sub-goals necessary to reach the overarching goal.
c. Make company goals, customer goals, vendor goals, and family goals.

STEP TWO:
Consider who is necessary to complete these goals.

a. Put the right person in the right seat. Keep in mind the Windfall Test, the 5Cs, and the 85/15 Test to help you determine where people should be.
b. Consider your role as a coach, mentor, spouse, parent, student, and leader.

STEP THREE:
Deploy the 50/50 Meeting to achieve your goals (group and one-on-ones).

a. First, show people how to be successful in their position by focusing on the four or five most important things.
b. Spend an equal amount of time talking about life.
c. Establish and live by your rules and core values.

A Note from Jud Boies about
BUSINESS GOALS

My mother instilled an incredible work ethic in me. I had a newspaper route, delivering the Oakland Tribune to over ninety homes daily, at eleven years old. I became a contractor at sixteen years old. I've started several businesses and seen some incredible successes and a few character-building failures. None of it became meaningful until I recognized how God was growing me, shaping me, and developing me to work for Him to advance His kingdom.

In the late 1990s, the foundation of the **Business Goals** program was developed out of a need to help my own business. Soon, so many companies came to me asking me to help deploy the same tools in their business that I had deployed in my own business. In 2003, I was encouraged to teach the **Business Goals** program as a full-time endeavor. Two years later, I was asked to deploy the same tools being used to help businesses in the Church. This laid the foundation for the **Church Goals** program as well.

In 2011, the senior pastor at the church I had been deeply involved in since 1997 called and asked me to become the executive pastor of the church's operations. God clearly wanted me to see the church from the inside and understand the intricacies of running and growing a church. During my nine years as Executive Pastor, we grew Bayside Church to one of the fastest-growing churches in America (ranked the #1 fastest-growing church in America by Outreach Magazine in 2019[5]). We helped thousands of other churches grow through our Thrive Conference, which we host every year. In 2020, we launched **Church Goals** and **Business Goals** as a full-time ministry of Thrive to help churches and pastors worldwide grow and become all that God desired for them to be. Since 2020, hundreds of churches and businesses have deployed the **Church Goals** and **Business Goals** programs…with remarkable success.

---

[5] 2019 Fastest-Growing Churches in America," Outreach Magazine, Outreach 100, https://outreach100.com/fastest-growing-churches-in-america/2019.

GETTING CONNECTED WITH THE BUSINESS GOALS PROGRAM

Connect with the **Business Goals** Program @ www.businessgoals.org or scan the QR code:

Sign up for a **Business Goals** class @ https://bit.ly/3Nj9frN or scan the QR code:

Connect with Jud Boies directly via email: **info@businessgoals.org.**

Follow us on social media:

https://www.facebook.com/BizGoals

https://twitter.com/goals_business

https://www.instagram.com/biz_goals/

https://www.linkedin.com/company/business-goals/